THE MOOD GUIDE
TO FABRIC AND FASHION

THE MOOD GUIDE TO FABRIC AND FASHION

The Essential Guide from the World's Most Famous Fabric Store

FOREWORD BY TIM GUNN

PHOTOGRAPHY BY JOHNNY MILLER

STC CRAFT / A MELANIE FALICK BOOK / NEW YORK

Mood's store in NYC's Garment District boasts 3 floors' worth of fabrics and trims. On a typical day, the store welcomes some 1,200 visitors, many of whom are personally greeted by founder Jack Sauma (bottom left), Swatch the dog, and Mood's team of fabric experts.

Published in 2015 by Stewart, Tabori & Chang An imprint of ABRAMS

Text © 2015 Mood Designer Fabrics Photographs © 2015 Johnny Miller (unless otherwise noted on page 174)

Library of Congress Control Number: 2014959131 ISBN: 978-1-61769-088-4

Editor: MELANIE FALICK Designer: MARY JANE CALLISTER Production Manager: DENISE LACONGO

The text of this book was composed in Miller, Futura, and Geotica Printed and bound in China. 10 9 8 7 6 5 4 3 2 1

Stewart, Tabori & Chang books are available at special discounts when purchased in quantity for premiums and promotions as well as fundraising or educational use. Special editions can also be created to specification. For details, contact specialsales@abramsbooks.com or the address below.

ABRAMS
THE ART OF BOOKS SINCE 1949

115 West 18th Street New York, NY 10011 www.abramsbooks.com

Foreword

Going to Mood Fabrics is like going to the Library of Congress of textiles. Any fabric you could possibly want is there, along with many you probably never knew existed. And every bolt of material has an educational experience woven into it. There's simply no place like it.

I discovered Mood and its owners—Eric, Phil, and Jack Sauma—in the fall of 2000, when I became Chair of the Department of Fashion Design at Parsons The New School for Design in New York. I had been tasked with repositioning the program for a new century, but as an administrator, I had little first-hand experience with garment sourcing and production. So I took a textile tour of New York's Garment District, and when I walked into Mood, I was spellbound. The variety, intricacy, and quality of the fabrics were like nothing I'd ever seen. Mood functions as a textile archive of sorts for the world's top designers—yet anyone can come in and buy a yard or two, and at a deep discount to boot. Why would you go anywhere else?

Believe it or not, when I arrived at Parsons, textile education wasn't part of the curriculum, which hadn't changed since the 1950s. Students made only prototype garments until their senior year, at which point they were placed under the tutelage of top New York designers. Those houses provided mentoring and leftover materials with which to make clothes (which were designed and evaluated according to the creative director's point of view). Frenzied scavenger hunts for the perfect novelty bouclé? Falling in love with a print and designing a collection around it? Not on the syllabus. And so, although the designer mentoring program was the crown jewel of the Parsons fashion department, one of my first actions as chair was to scrap it—I wanted to get students out into the world, learning about and sourcing fabric as hands-on creators.

I was terrified that my decision might get me fired, but the students were ecstatic. And Mood was (and still is) their best resource. When you're on a student budget and you're buying a three-ply cashmere that Michael Kors had ordered and didn't use all of, you're getting a bargain. And there's something quite thrilling about knowing that you're working with a fabric that was in the Marc Jacobs showroom, or Diane von Furstenberg's, or Oscar de la Renta's. As a young designer, you're embracing a legacy, so to speak. If you were a young filmmaker, it would be like filming on Steven Spielberg's set.

Taking students to Mood to learn about and shop for fabric was part of my greater objective at Parsons: to help students cultivate their own creative visions. Fashion doesn't live on paper or as a muslin prototype; fabric is as essential as form in creating a cohesive, wearable, and desirable collection. Anyone who wishes to create beautiful clothes—or wear them—owes it to him or herself to learn as much as he or she can about the world of fabric. As for me, it was an honor to roll up my sleeves and give Parsons fashion students the skills they really needed—not just to get a job, but to lead an industry. And I will proudly tell you that the first graduating class of this new curriculum included Jack McCollough and Lazaro Hernandez of Proenza Schouler.

I'd been taking my students to Mood for a few years when I was approached by the producers of a top-secret reality-TV pilot called *Project Runway*. None of us had any idea whether the show would even make it to the air, much less become the cultural touchstone it is today. We were all donating our time. My role was that of a consultant; there wasn't a "me" on the show. And no one believed it was possible when I suggested we give the contestants a design challenge to complete in one day. But then we did a test run using some

Parsons students in place of contestants, and I took them to Mood to shop. The next thing I knew, I was going there with my campers and the cameras were rolling! But I have to tell you, the entire time we were taping that first season, I never dreamed I'd end up in the cut of the show. Now, many years later, the show is in sixty countries, and people from all over the world flock to Mood—and sometimes not even to buy fabric, but to take tourist snapshots and catch a glimpse of Swatch the dog. We're big in Finland? Who knew?

One marvelous result of the *Project Runway* phenomenon—and the newfound fame of Mood—is an explosion of interest in fashion careers and sewing in general. When I took over the fashion program at Parsons, there were two hundred students. When I left in 2007, there were close to six hundred, and now there are more than 1,000. Fashion enrollments all over the nation have grown. And so, in turn, has Mood. I certainly have had a very ancillary role in its transformation from mom-and-pop fabric shop to renowned retail brand, but it's been wonderful to be a spectator. When I first started visiting Mood, the store had one floor; now it has three. It stocks notions and trims for one-stop shopping. It has opened a Los Angeles location that's become a tremendous educational

resource for that community, as well as a terrific e-commerce site. It's been leading the way in offering new technologies in textiles. And one of the reasons it's such a delight to keep returning is that the team are so lovely to work with. The staffers are a tremendously knowledgeable resource, and many of them are designers themselves. The Saumas are sweethearts with entrepreneurship in their DNA (see Chapter 1), and with the ongoing development of Mood's web site, online and in-store education programs, and social media platforms—and now this book— I foresee total world domination!

When one of my *Project Runway* designers has a question about fabric, I send him or her straight to the mother ship. Think of these pages as an extension of the legendary store. Like Mood itself, the book is more than a functional textile resource; it's a fount of inspiration and wisdom, full of fashion history, design ideas, and the sort of offhand, you-won't-learn-this-in-class tips that come from decades of experience on the front lines of fashion. I'm thrilled that Mood and the Sauma family are leveraging their expertise to educate people and encourage them to dream and create. I look forward to watching a new generation of designers make it work.

—TIM GUNN

Introduction

The New York fashion industry may seem glamorous, but the neighborhood where it all comes together is surprisingly down to earth. Mere blocks from the glass-and-neon glow of Times Square, the Parisian elegance of Bryant Park, and the austere galleries and chic boîtes of Chelsea is the Garment District— the last bastion of manufacturing in gentrified modern-day Manhattan. Here, function trumps fuss and inspiration gets down to business.

Turn-of-the-century brick office towers, dusted by decades'-worth of diesel smoke, house working garment factories stacked high in the sky. Scattered among them are showrooms, design studios, and tiny sample rooms, where patternmakers carve out and refine the shapes for next season's runways. At street level, look out! Young men wheel garment racks toward idling trucks and FedEx vans, ready to deliver the merch to Barneys or Bloomingdale's. Industrial storage bins, stuffed with disassembled mannequins or bolts of jersey, lurk in doorways. The shops are fantastically specific: Some sell only sewing machines, while others focus on zippers or ribbons. A few storefronts, peddling flashy clothing in curiously un-flashy atmospheres, read TO THE TRADE ONLY: Merchants from Eastern Europe or Africa might stop there to stock up on wholesale clothes for their boutiques, and curious visitors aren't allowed. You might catch a model or a particularly glamorous fashion student zipping by, but the atmosphere isn't quite that of a sidewalk fashion show. For one thing, everyone's in too much of a hurry.

The north side of 37th Street just west of Seventh Avenue seems especially bustling. A steady stream of visitors passes through the doorway of No. 225 and into two old-fashioned hand-cranked elevators, manned by uniformed operators just like in *Mad Men*. Making this daily pilgrimage are fashion designers, tourists, the odd supermodel, people speaking Hebrew and Spanish and Mandarin and Tagalog. "Mood?" asks the operator. "Yes," the passengers inevitably say, "Mood." It's the only reason many people brave the Garment District in the first place— and the only fabric store in the world that's as famous as the designers it serves.

Mood Fabrics is more than a place to buy materials for sewing; it's a living archive of the world's most extraordinary designer textiles, straight from the world's most pres-

Above: Shelves of silk at Mood's NYC store. Fabrics at Mood, like fabrics in this book, are organized by fiber content.

and a one-of-a-kind charmeuse panel digitally printed with a painting by the couturier Ralph Rucci, you might find a harried intern gathering swatches of crepe de chine for her boss, Oscar de la Renta. A pair of wildly styled Parsons students, speaking rapid-fire Japanese, scan the denim shelves in preparation for a class project. A group of preteens enrolled in fashion design camp sit on the stairs, sketching styles and dreaming about becoming the next Phoebe Philo or Alexander Wang. Past and present *Project Runway* designers make daily pit stops at Mood; one, Kooan Kosuke from Season 10, even works here. A Tim Gunn sighting causes such a ruckus that it can block the entrance to the store. And any given cutting table might be shared with a celebrity (Beyoncé, Katie Holmes, Sarah Jessica Parker), which might be why a sizable minority of visitors are tourists who've never so much as touched a sewing machine. Meandering through the store as he keeps an eye on it all is Swatch the Boston terrier, Mood's store mascot and most popular employee.

tigious showrooms and factory shelves. The sheer spectacle of so much beautiful fabric piled together in one place is part of the reason that more than 1,200 people visit the New York City store alone every day. In the silk department, near metallic brocades fresh from Carolina Herrera's sample room

Twenty-eight hundred miles away, on a sun-baked stretch of South La Brea Avenue, the Los Angeles outpost of Mood is just as lively (though in this spread-out city, the wide-open retail space still manages to feel serene).

> ## "It's a mecca now. People from all over the world come to see it, and we're happy to welcome them."
>
> —JACK SAUMA

Mood branched out to L.A. in 2007 when *Project Runway* did, and immediately became a go-to resource for the film and TV industries and the city's burgeoning community of fashion designers and sewers. Thanks to its roomy floor plan, it also has the space to host classes almost every day for thousands of students a year. Today, a dozen sewing newbies—one instantly recognizable Hollywood character actress among them—sit at their professional-grade machines as they stitch up customized tote bags. Seized by inspiration, one student dashes over to the Interior Fabrics section to snap up some brocade for an accent panel. She nearly bumps into a world-renowned interior designer perusing heavy jacquards for reupholstering a celebrity client's sofa. Across the room, a costume designer for *Game of Thrones* is scoring the perfect silk for an elaborate dress for Daenearys. And yes, there's a canine Mood mascot roaming the aisles here, too—he's a Chihuahua named, appropriately enough, Oscar.

Together with moodfabrics.com, the Mood outposts sell more than a million yards (900,000 meters) of fabric each year—roughly enough to stretch from New York to Detroit, or Paris to Milan. With influence like this, Mood is as much fashion epicenter as fabric store, and its owners and employees are privy to the secrets of some of the world's most influential design minds. This book is part of Mood's greater mission: to share this wealth of resources and experience by empowering fashion and sewing enthusiasts to make the most of their creativity.

Alongside the inspiring story of the Sauma family—whose patriarch, Jack, founded Mood in 1990 after decades spent in the fashion industry and shares the business with his sons today—the following chapters introduce you to Mood's expert sales staff and roster of designer friends, who share tips on how to shop for fabrics and create inspired designs. Phil Sauma offers a peek into his world, taking you on a trip to the Gandini textile showroom in Milan (Chanel and Valentino's go-to source) and explaining what makes a fabric good (and a good value). And for every type of fabric, from cotton to cashmere, the book delves deep into the Mood vault for the details on its unique properties and design potential, and how to work with its quirks. Whether or not you live near a Mood store (and there's always moodfabrics.com if you don't), this book has the tools you need to understand fabric and design with confidence. It's the Saumas' goal to have every project finish with the words made famous by *Project Runway*: "Thank you, Mood!"

The Fabric of Their Lives

Mood Fabrics has all the elements of a classic American success story: an odyssey of oppression and emigration spanning three continents; a dash of true love; a splash of runway glamour; and years of blood, sweat, and tears. It's a family business in the truest sense of the term—and fabric and fashion are embedded in the Sauma family's DNA. Founder Jack Sauma is the son of fabric vendors; he now owns and operates Mood with his own sons,

Above: Brothers Phillip and Eric Sauma on 37th Street in New York City, just outside the entrance to Mood.

Phillip and Eric. Jack's wife Janet is descended from a long line of tailors; she and her daughter Amy, while currently less involved on a day-to-day basis, have both spent years helping to build the business. The family's tale is every bit as inspiring as the designer textiles on Mood's shelves.

FOUNDATIONS

Jack Sauma was born in 1951 in the Mesopotamian capital of Hassake (Al-Hasakah), Syria, where his father owned a small fabric shop in the city center. Seven years later, Syria merged with Egypt to form the short-lived United Arab Republic; Egyptians flooded into Syria, igniting tensions with locals and especially with the Assyrian Christian ethnic group to which the Saumas belonged. When a group of Egyptian soldiers

stormed into the store and one spit in the elder Sauma's face, the family fled to Lebanon the next day. There, young Jack was sent to a monastery. Nine years later, the Saumas were among the first hundred or so Assyrians to receive asylum in politically neutral Sweden through the World Council of Churches.

In Stockholm, the senior Saumas found their niche operating ready-to-wear factories, overseeing cutting, sewing, and finishing for Scandinavian fashion designers. Teenaged Jack, observing the process from start to finish, resolved to make his way into the creative side of the industry. "I figured, why should my family work for other people when I could be the guy to sell my product?" he recalls. And so, after high school, he enrolled in the design program at Stockholm's prestigious Anders Beckmans Skola (now Beckmans Designhögskola). His graduation collection in 1974 caused a veritable sensation. Reporters and photographers from local papers came to cover it; store buyers were intrigued. "It was the Gatsby look," Jack says. "High-end sportswear, velvets, cottons, denims." H&M—at the time, a department store that sold clothing from outside labels—snapped up the entire range, and a business was born. "I thought I'd be making maybe two or three hundred pieces to start," Jack says. "It was more like forty, fifty thousand."

Yves Saint Laurent. Givenchy. Dior. Jack Sauma of Sweden. At boutiques and department stores throughout northern Europe, Sauma's fledgling label hung alongside fashion's best and brightest. "I was young and

Previous pages: Mood's New York store reflects the vision of founder Jack Sauma (bottom right, with his wife Janet), who got his start as a fashion designer in Sweden before owning clothing lines and a garment factory in New York.

very happy about it," Jack recalls with characteristic understatement. His spectacular early run as a designer took a detour, however, on a family trip to Istanbul. On a previous trip there, Jack's mother had met, through a priest, a beautiful young Assyrian woman named Janet—the daughter of a tailor and the perfect bride, she was convinced, for her son. Jack was dubious. "That was the old tradition, and I said, 'I will never, ever do this,'" he remembers. "But I went to Istanbul just for fun. And it was love at first sight." Janet's brothers were tailors in New York's Garment District, and the young couple flew in for a visit. After the ambitious Jack had a taste of the Big Apple, there was no turning back. He married Janet in New Jersey, shut down Jack Sauma of Sweden, and in 1976, they moved to New York.

The Saumas set up house on Long Island, where in the late '70s and early '80s their children, Phillip, Amy, and Eric, were born. Jack trained his sights on the fashion industry, where he'd try his luck as a sewing contractor for other designers, just as his parents had done before him. The new business was called La Mouche Sportswear—"because I had a moustache," he says, playfully outlining the shape on his now-clean-shaven face. Though he had few connections when he arrived in the big city, Jack quickly became a popular guy. His client list (and group of friends) grew to include the crème de la crème of New York fashion: Norma Kamali, Geoffrey Beene, Giorgio di Sant'Angelo, and Pierre Cardin, to name just a few designers.

(The Sauma kids were along for the ride, hanging out after school and on weekends and doing their homework on the cutting-room floor. "We'd have swordfights with the cardboard tubes of fabric rolls," remembers Phillip.) Buoyed by La Mouche's success, Jack went on to launch several successful clothing lines of his own, such as Isaiah and Joyce Jordan. From Bergdorf's to Bloomingdale's to Bendel's, "my clothing was in every window," he says.

JACK'S SECOND ACT

It was a golden era for New York fashion—until the economy came to a screeching halt with the stock-market crash of October 1987. Customers stopped shopping, department stores slid into bankruptcy, and Jack grew increasingly frustrated waiting for payments that never came. In search of a new revenue stream, he began selling old fabrics from his collection to wholesale customers, and was surprised at how quickly he recouped his investment. "It worked like 1-2-3," Jack says. He reached out to his famous friends and former clients, offering to buy their leftover fabric, and the operation quickly took over the Saumas' lives. "Our basement, garage, and storage barn were filled with fabric," recalls Eric of his childhood. "We all helped out. My father would sell it by the pound, by the suitcase, anything to just flip it."

The success of this new venture prompted Jack to find a permanent home in the Garment District for Mood Designer Fabrics, which opened its doors in 1991 at 250 West

> **"Our basement, garage, and storage barn were filled with fabric. We all helped out. My father would sell it by the pound, by the suitcase, anything to just flip it."**
>
> —ERIC SAUMA

Favorite fabric:
"Anything with a textured, fuzzy feel"—faux fur, polar fleece—"because it resembles his bed," says owner Eric Sauma.

He may not be the most helpful Mood employee, but Swatch the Boston terrier is certainly the most beloved. Owner Eric Sauma estimates that 100 visitors per day come to the New York store solely to take photos of Swatch, who shot to fame on *Project Runway* and now models outfits on the Sewciety blog on Mood's web site. Fans bring him chew toys and treats ("That's why he's a little on the pudgy side," says Eric) and have sewn him leather jackets, raincoats, leashes, and collars. Mood is a dog-friendly store, and Swatch has a way of rounding up packs and leading them around.

Swatch is also smart: He's capable of riding the elevator by himself from the third floor to the eleventh floor, home of Mood's sister wholesale business, Preview Textile. (If the elevator stops before the eleventh floor, or before the third floor on its way down, he won't get out.) Ever the diplomatic salesperson, Swatch also can sense when a customer is afraid of him, and will retreat behind the counter to make that person more comfortable. If he's not trotting around the sales floor, he can usually be found during lunch hour in the break room, waiting for crumbs to fall, or napping on the floor, legs peeking out from beneath the fabric shelves. Says Eric: "He's a boy inside of a dog's body."

Opposite: Mood is a resource for designers, who come to swatch fabrics for their collections under the watchful eye of Swatch the dog.

39th Street, on the tenth floor. Thousands of fabric rolls were lugged up the elevator and onto the shelves by young Phillip and his friends, high-school freshmen at the time. (As for the name? It came from one of Jack's many '80s clothing lines.) In the early years, Mood was strictly a fabric wholesaler; when fashion-conscious home sewers came knocking, they were politely turned away. Sensing an opportunity, Janet Sauma decided in 1993 to spearhead an expansion into retail sales. Word about the fabric store with the best stock steadily spread—thanks in no small part to the efforts of the Sauma boys. "We would stand on the streets in the Garment District holding fliers and shouting, 'Fabric sale! Fabric sale! Finest fabrics you can find, on the tenth floor,'" recalls Eric, who was twelve when enlisted for the job. "We'd take girls by the hand and walk them up to the store. They would see a cute little kid and say, 'OK, I'll trust this kid.' They'd come up and have a great experience and tell other people about it, and that's what built the retail end of our business. Hard work does pay off."

Mood kept expanding its footprint until there was nowhere left to go in the building, and in 2001, the store moved into its current location at 225 West 37th Street, with 40,000 square feet spread out over three floors. A second location debuted in Los Angeles in 2007, serving not only designers and home sewers but also the Hollywood film and television industry, whose creative talents frequent the store to costume their casts and whip up Oscar gowns from the finest silks in the West.

The large classroom area inside hosts top-of-the-line sewing equipment and a roster of top costumers and designers teaching daily classes—almost like a mini-university for the local crafter community.

THE PROJECT RUNWAY REVOLUTION

In 2002, a small production crew walked into Mood on 37th Street and asked the Saumas about filming the pilot for a TV reality show inside the store. "They looked like kids," recalls Eric. "We'd done photo shoots in the store before, so we figured, why not?" *Project Runway* instantly became one of the most successful reality shows of all time, introducing phrases like "Make it work!" and "Thank you, Mood" into the vernacular and inspiring a generation of viewers to pursue fashion careers or simply try their hand at sewing. Mood—and its dizzying array of fine fabrics,

trims, and notions—became an indispensable resource for the contestants, and the breakout star of the show. By the third season, paparazzi would camp out outside the store during filming. "It's a mecca now," says Jack. "People from all over the world come to see it, and we're happy to welcome them." In fact, some of the hundreds of tourists who pop into the New York City store each day don't even sew; they're simply hoping to catch a glimpse of Tim Gunn, Swatch the dog, or one of the many *Project Runway* alumni who now call the store their inspirational second home.

DESTINATION SHOPPING, TODAY AND TOMORROW

Jack still commutes every day to Mood, where he holds court at the glass table near the entrance to the store—that is, if he's not running around, chatting up customers and

Left to right: Heidi Klum and Tim Gunn during *Project Runway* Season 12; Sean Kelley at Mood during *Project Runway* Season 13.

old friends. But now his adult sons have equally important roles in the business. Phillip Sauma goes on buying trips to textile mills in Italy, France, Germany, and Belgium each month, and designers like Carolina Herrera, Ralph Lauren, and Marc Jacobs call him first when they have fabric left over from a production run. Phil studied textiles at The Fashion Institute of Technology and has a knack for sussing out styles that satisfy his customers'—and the fashion industry's—evolving tastes. He also has a sixth sense when it comes to the fabrics themselves. Most industry veterans still set a swatch on fire to see what it's made of (animal fibers smell like hair; synthetics melt). "I can pretty much tell the composition of a fabric with my fingertips," Phil says.

Eric's role is to oversee the nuts and bolts of business operations: streamlining inventory systems, running the numbers, staffing the stores. (He's also recognizable from *Project Runway*, more so than his camera-shy older brother.) But if there's one thing the Saumas have learned as a family, it's the importance of wearing many hats. "All of us do everything," says Eric. "There's no such thing as 'that's my brother's job' or 'that's my mom's job.' If I'm away and he needs to run the store, he can do it. We all overlap. Because we've got to make it work for the customers."

Under the younger Saumas' direction, Mood is adapting to a changing world. Not only do the brothers keep on top of the textile industry, but they continue to find new ways to nurture the fashion and crafting communities through in-store classes and workshops and, coming soon, online courses free to all. Moodfabrics.com functions as an extension of Mood's inventory for customers worldwide. The site is also a hub of inspiration where aspiring designers and home sewers can gather ideas from the Mood blog, read about the creations of the bloggers of the Mood Sewing Network, and create their own image-rich Mood Boards. Tens of thousands of style-philes worldwide track the Mood team's fashion-week activities and visual references on Instagram and Pinterest. And new retail stores are in the planning stages—both in the United States and abroad.

With five Sauma grandchildren and counting—Amy's three kids live with her in London; Phil's older son and daughter, as New Yorkers, are already frequent visitors to the store—Mood might just stay the Sauma show for generations to come. "I tell my son he can do whatever he wants," says Phil. "But when you get your feet wet, you realize a sense of pride and potential. You want to build on it. Not just for yourself, but for your family."

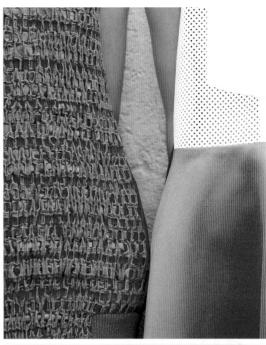

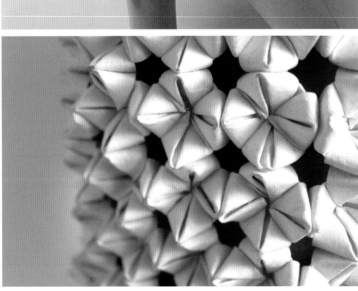

Social Fabric TEXTILES YESTERDAY, TODAY, AND TOMORROW

Fabric has played a crucial role in human history. As humans learned to cover their bodies, they became mobile, spreading and intermingling civilizations around the world; as they learned to adorn their garments, windows, and walls, fabric has informed the growth of art and culture. The desire for beautiful new fabrics, notably silk, paved the way for the growth of entire empires. Textiles have functioned throughout history as a social differentiator. Silk was once reserved for emperors and is now on the racks in every fast-fashion chain store, while the rough, chunky textures once reserved for the backs of laborers can today be found in high fashion. Today, the textile industry continues to exist on the forefront of cultural development, breaking new ground in the realms of technology and environmental sustainability. Fabric is everywhere, and a part of everything.

FABRICS OF THE FUTURE

"Fabric has changed so much in the last ten years; it's mind-blowing," says Phil Sauma. Microfibers have given rise to synthetic silks, jerseys, and fleeces of unprecedented softness and lightness. Nanotechnology can make fabrics resist stains or wrinkles, block ultraviolet light or hazardous chemicals, or even impart aloe vera into the skin. "Smart" clothing, a growing field of research and development, researches ways in which textile fibers can conduct electrical signals for a variety of benefits: lighting up for safety, keeping the wearer warm, even playing music. The book *Extreme Textiles*, published in conjunction with the exhibition at the Cooper-Hewitt National Design Museum (see timeline on page 33), is a terrific exploration of the possibilities for fabric's future: Textiles can be found in everything from knitted replacement heart valves to synthetic skin grafts. Woven carbon fiber is used to supplement automotive and aircraft construction and could even be used someday to build skyscrapers.

Above: It may look like embroidered lace, but this garment from threeASFOUR's spring/summer 2014 collection is made from a variety of laser-cut silks. New technologies are creating never-before-seen effects in fabric.

EARTH MATTERS:
SUSTAINABILITY AND FABRIC

In recent years, fashion, like other industries, has turned its eye to **sustainability**—lightening the impact of garment production on people and the planet so that the industry can sustain itself given the world's limited supply of natural resources. Fabric is an important part of this equation, though it's far from the only facet of the fashion industry that leaves room for improvement. (Human rights in the sewing labor force is a related concern that's rightly gaining momentum in the public consciousness.)

The factors addressed below affect the impact of a fabric's production process on the environment. Most fabric mills are fairly

Previous pages: Fabric takes many forms. Clockwise from top left: One of Paco Rabanne's chain-mail creations as shown in the April 1966 issue of *Mademoiselle*; a detail of technical fabrics from Sacai's spring 2014 collection showing laminated, woven, and laser cut fabrics; fashion's take on the traditional kimono as shown in the July 1970 issue of *Vogue*; origami folded fabric from Elena Salmistraro.

opaque about their sourcing—which means that as a retail fabric shopper and home sewer, there might not be much you can do to go green, short of buying organic fabric itself. Country of origin matters, too; fabric produced in Western Europe or the United States must follow stricter environmental regulations than fabric from emerging Asian markets. The best approach is to keep in mind the quality and the life cycle of a garment: The longer a style lasts, the less needless junk you'll buy to replace it.

FIBER ORIGIN AND METHOD OF PRODUCTION. Cotton generates more pesticide use than any crop in the world, and requires large amounts of water in its cultivation. Animal fibers and leather come from farm animals, which require land and food, and expel greenhouse gases from their digestive systems. Some materials (cotton, wool, silk) sold to designers come certified organic by various third parties (see page 27), which can mean that they are grown without pesticides or genetic modification, processed without toxic chemicals, produced with regard to energy efficiency, or some combination thereof. Many other fabrics claim to be organic but are not labeled with any certification; still others come from recycled content (either recycled from cutting-room scraps or from post-industrial or post-consumer material). Generally speaking, organic fabrics are harder to come by in a retail store than they are for design houses, which usually special-order them from mills and converters (a business that customizes untreated fabrics made by other mills,

through dyeing, texturizing, and so on; see page 51). The organic fabrics that trickle down to Mood represent a small piece of the pie. Phil notes that some of the organic cottons sold at Mood come undyed and unprocessed. "Be sure you preshrink them before cutting and sewing," he says, "because they haven't always been treated and finished in the same way as other fabrics."

ENERGY REQUIRED TO PRODUCE THE FIBER, YARN, AND FABRIC. While bamboo rayon comes from the easily regenerated and therefore environmentally sustainable bamboo plant (so fast-growing it's considered an

Above: A dress made from organic Japanese cotton twill and traditional Philippine pineapple fiber fabric by Titiana Inglis. Designers are increasingly turning to more eco-conscious materials.

> "What I find modern is the balanced use of both traditional fabrics and new textiles. It's the idea of combining well-known quality with new surfaces that makes them exciting."
>
> —HELMUT LANG

agricultural pest), it requires large amounts of energy to break down the tough bamboo shoots into cellulose to be spun into fiber. The same problem applies to recycled polyester. In Phillip Sauma's opinion, because of its energy consumption, recycled polyester has little to no net environmental benefit; some designers and companies, however, believe otherwise. Patagonia, for instance, collects used polar-fleece jackets, then sends them to a mill in Japan, which breaks the jackets down into polyester fiber to make new fabric.

At the low-tech end of the spectrum, some fabrics, generally those from India,

Above: Sustainable fabrics are increasingly high-tech. This look from Issey Miyake's fall/winter 2013 men's collection utilized a material made from recycled plastic water bottles that retains heat and resists wind.

are still **hand-loomed**; this means they are produced without electricity. Mood and most other fabric stores don't generally carry much of this fabric, as it's produced in small lots on demand, but if you're able to track such fabric down, it can be beautiful in look and texture.

IMPACT OF DYES AND FINISHES ON WATER, AIR, AND WORKER HEALTH. Some **dyestuffs** and **finishing chemicals** used to break down or refine the feel of a fabric can contain toxic and carcinogenic compounds—such as phthalates and formaldehyde—which can be discharged into waterways, harming fish, wildlife, and human health. (There's a saying—sad but sometimes true—that you can tell which colors will be in style next season by looking at the rivers in China.) This information is sometimes, but not always, supplied to designers who order the fabric, but it rarely makes its way to the shelves of a fabric store. Generally speaking, if a textile smells like chemicals, it probably contains them.

Some fabrics—namely, Tencel or lyocell—use what's called a **closed-loop system** in which processing chemicals are reused and kept inside the factory rather than flushed into the water supply. Because Tencel is also made from renewable eucalyptus, it's generally considered a sustainable fabric.

Environmental laws are strictest in Western Europe and the United States, so fabrics that originate in those places should have been produced with reasonable air and water pollution controls in place. Mood sells home dye kits that meet United States standards for

TYPES OF ORGANIC AND SUSTAINABLE FABRIC CERTIFICATION

Most fabrics sold in retail stores won't be labeled with certification, but it's good to familiarize yourself with the third-party organizations that are working to audit and label various fibers and textiles for organic, non-toxic, and sustainable properties.

GLOBAL ORGANIC TEXTILE STANDARD (GOTS) Fabrics must have at least 70% organic content and be processed and dyed in a manner that meets environmental sustainability criteria.

OEKO-TEX STANDARD The Standard 100 label refers to the purity of the textile itself, which is tested for an array of toxic substances. Fabrics labeled OEKO-TEX Standard 1000 have also been audited for environmental and social sustainability at all stages of the production process.

BLUESIGN This certification comes after a comprehensive evaluation of a fabric's sustainability, including everything from the social and environmental impact of the raw material to the mill's energy efficiency and water and air emissions.

> "The greenest thing you could do in fashion is to buy something great that you're going to use for years."
>
> —MICHAEL KORS

what can go down the drain. **Natural dyes** such as indigo are surging in popularity; some crafters order naturally derived powders and kits from such sites as Etsy.com, while others simply use purple cabbage, onion skins, or tea. "I've been to mills in China where they're dyeing organic cotton," says Phil, "and let me tell you, there's nothing organic or healthy about the dye they're using."

ELIMINATION OF PRODUCTION WASTE. By reclaiming unwanted excess yardage that would otherwise go to waste, Mood helps to maximize the efficiency of the fabric supply chain. Likewise, by buying and sewing fabric that's already been produced for someone else, a customer at a store like Mood isn't creating any new demand for resources. Among fashion designers, **a zero-waste movement** is taking root; proponents advocate eliminating cutting-floor waste, whether through more efficient pattern layouts or reuse of scraps.

CARBON FOOTPRINT OF SHIPPING METHODS. How far has the fabric come? "Some fabrics are woven with Chinese yarn, dyed and finished in Italy, then shipped to factories in Asia to be sewn into garments," says Phil. That's a lot of mileage—and a lot of petroleum fuel required for all those container ships and trucks. While it's difficult for a retail customer to track the provenance of fabrics that far back, it's certainly worth thinking about.

LIFE CYCLE OF THE FABRIC AND GARMENT ITSELF. Opting for quality over quantity is as important as what kind of fabric you choose. A garment made lovingly at home in a beautiful, high-quality fabric will get more mileage in your wardrobe than ten cheap, sweatshop-made designer knockoffs from the mall (even if they're certified organic). This, too, is what sustainability is all about.

Fabrics are like people: You can often tell
a lot about them by where they're from.
Some countries and regions of the world
are known for their quality and design,
while others specialize in specific types of
fabric. Here is a map of fabric-producing
countries and what they're known for.

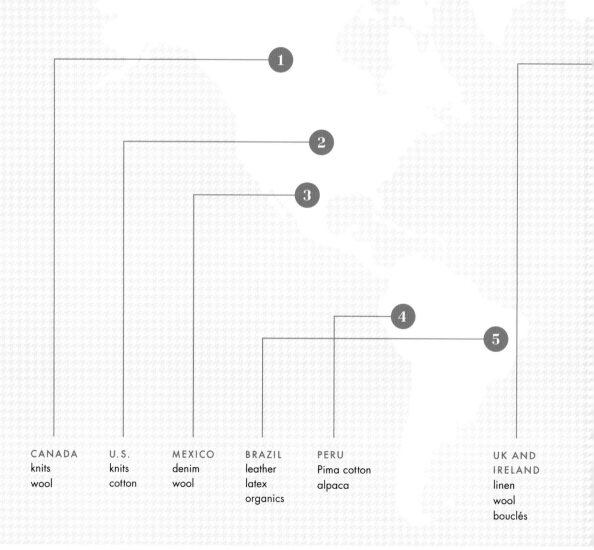

CANADA
knits
wool

U.S.
knits
cotton

MEXICO
denim
wool

BRAZIL
leather
latex
organics

PERU
Pima cotton
alpaca

UK AND
IRELAND
linen
wool
bouclés

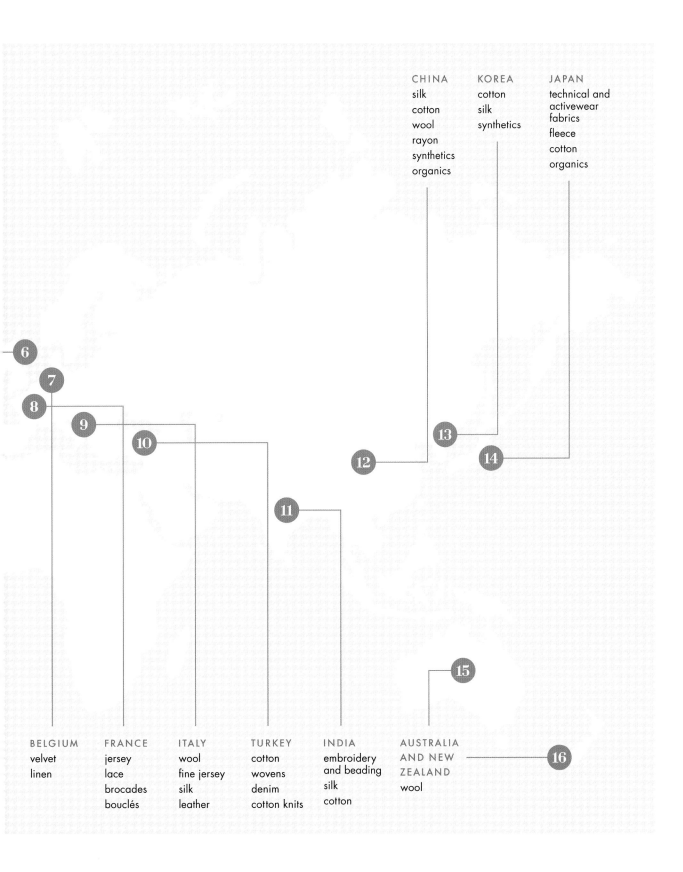

CHINA
silk
cotton
wool
rayon
synthetics
organics

KOREA
cotton
silk
synthetics

JAPAN
technical and
activewear
fabrics
fleece
cotton
organics

BELGIUM
velvet
linen

FRANCE
jersey
lace
brocades
bouclés

ITALY
wool
fine jersey
silk
leather

TURKEY
cotton
wovens
denim
cotton knits

INDIA
embroidery
and beading
silk
cotton

AUSTRALIA
AND NEW
ZEALAND
wool

The history of fabric reflects the history of humanity itself. Here, a guide to some major milestones in the technology and culture of textiles.

PREHISTORY
The earliest humans protected and insulated their bodies with pelts of fur or animal hides.

6500 B.C.
Artifacts found in Turkey indicate the use of felt, created from the mashing together of fibers. Artifacts found in Israel indicate the use of naalbinding, an early textile-making technique (a cousin to crochet) involving short lengths of yarn.

5000 B.C.
Linen, reed, and papyrus fabrics are woven in Egypt.

4200 B.C.
Naalbinding artifacts in Denmark indicate the spread of textile-making to northern Europe. (The name comes from the Danish word for needle.)

500 B.C.
Chain mail—interlocking metal rings forming a textile—is used by the Celts as body armor.

200 B.C.
Early evidence reveals the advent of needle knitting among indigenous Peruvians.

200 B.C. TO 1000 A.D.
The Silk Road—actually a collection of trade routes—develops and thrives. Trade in silk and dyes, among other goods, fosters the spread of art, ideas, and religions between civilizations in Asia and Europe. The Ottoman and Roman empires rise and fall, and the bubonic plague spreads through these routes. Silk becomes a luxury good in Europe.

56 A.D.
Seneca the Younger attempts to ban the wearing of silk in the Roman Senate, declaring it "[does] not hide the body, nor even one's decency."

200
Woodblock textile printing takes place in China.

276
The wife of Emperor Aurelian orders a silk dress whose cost would have made it literally worth its weight in gold. (Aurelian, outraged, cancels the order.)

300
With the mollusk *Purpura*—whose mucus is the source of purple dye—threatened with extinction, Byzantine emperor Theodosius decrees that only the royal family may wear the color purple.

500 TO 1000
The spinning wheel is invented in India.

700
Batik dye technique is invented in China.

1000
Cotton socks are knitted in Egypt.

1519
Spanish conquistadores Pizarro and Cortez discover cotton in Central and South America, and introduce it to Europe.

1589
British clergyman William Lee invents the stocking frame, a hand-operated knitting machine. According to legend, he created the machine because a woman he was courting was more interested in knitting than in him.

1733
British inventor John Kay patents the flying shuttle, paving the way for industrialized textile production.

1774
Swedish chemist Carl Wilhelm Scheele discovers that chlorine removes color from fabric.

1784
The power loom is created by British inventor Edmund Cartwright.

1785
Roller printing is invented, launching industrial-scale fabric printing.

1801

French weaver Joseph Marie Jacquard invents the jacquard punch-card loom, allowing for the rapid weaving of intricate patterns within a textile.

1829

The first widely used sewing machine is invented by Barthélemy Thimmonier, a French tailor. The following year he opens the first machine-based sewing factory to manufacture French army uniforms; it is burned down by tailors fearful of losing their livelihood.

1844

John Mercer, a British fabric chemist and printer, patents the mercerization process, which gives cotton and linen textiles greater dye absorption, tensile strength, and sheen.

1856

William Perkin, an 18-year-old chemistry student in London, accidentally discovers the first synthetic dye when an attempt to synthesize quinine results in a vivid purple liquid.

1892

The viscose process is patented by a team of British scientists, paving the way for rayon and other silk substitutes.

1903

The first American fashion show takes place at Ehrlich Brothers department store in New York.

1935

DuPont invents nylon. It is first used for women's stockings, which had previously been made of silk.

1950

Orlon acrylic, a wool substitute, begins production at a DuPont facility in South Carolina.

1953

DuPont puts Dacron polyester fiber into production, marketing it as a wrinkle-free alternative to cotton and other natural fibers.

1955

James Dean stars in *Rebel Without a Cause*, cementing blue jeans' status as the official garment of cool.

1959
Spandex (also called elastane or Lycra®) is invented, paving the way for stretch fabrics and revolutionizing the fashion industry.

LATE 1960s
Spanish-born, Paris-based designer Paco Rabanne becomes famous for chain-mail dresses and accessories.

1968
For the first time in history, Americans consume more synthetic textiles than natural-fiber ones.

1970
Japanese chemist Miyoshi Okamoto invents Ultrasuede, a synthetic microfiber that resembles suede.

1977
Saturday Night Fever immortalizes the polyester leisure suit.

1990
British designer Katharine Hamnett, famous for her political statement T-shirts, begins to speak out on environmental issues, launching a campaign to raise awareness about the dangers of pesticides in cotton together with the Pesticide Action Network.

1992
Tencel (lyocell) is invented by Austrian company Lenzing using a closed-loop process that keeps solvents out of the water supply, making Tencel one of the first original sustainable fabrics.

1994
Patagonia's board votes to phase out the use of non-organic cotton in its products by 1996.

1996
Woody Harrelson plants four hemp seeds in Kentucky to bring awareness to the benefits of hemp fiber and that state's laws criminalizing its agriculture. He is immediately arrested. (Charges are eventually dismissed—in 2007.)

2005
The Cooper-Hewitt National Design Museum hosts the Extreme Textiles exhibition. Highlights include light switches made of pom-poms, a musical rope installation, and textiles for use in medicine and space travel.

2008
Speedo's LZR Racer suit for swimmers, made of a woven synthetic material designed to mimic shark skin and reduce drag in the water, results in 23 world records being broken at the Beijing Olympics.

Fabric 101

Shopping for fabric is sheer fun. Sometimes you'll want to simply stroll the store's aisles for hours to see what inspires you; other times, you might have a specific pattern or design in mind and need a fabric to fit the bill. But before it comes time to make real choices at the cutting table and cash register, it is helpful if you understand the fundamental properties of fabric: how it's made, how it behaves when used in different

YARN is the collection of fibers twisted together to form the strand used to knit or weave the body of a fabric (or a knitted or crocheted garment). THREAD is similar in that it's also a collection of twisted fibers, but this term refers to the strand used in a sewing machine (or hand-sewing needle) to stitch sections of fabric together. You buy thread for your sewing machine. Yarn is what makes up a fabric—the term doesn't just refer to a ball of wooly string used for knitting cozy gloves, though it can be that, too.

ways, and how much of it you will need to create a design. Of course, the Mood staff is always standing by to help!

FIBER AND YARN

The **fiber** is the raw material of the fabric. Wool, cotton, and polyester are types of fibers. The fibers are spun into **yarns**, which are then knitted or woven to form the fabric itself. Some fabrics are **blends**, made from more than one type of fiber. The **composition** refers to the percentages of various fibers constituting a fabric. In a store, this information should be marked on or near every roll.

WOVEN, KNIT, OR NEITHER?

Most fabrics fall into one of two categories: wovens or knits. This classification is the most important thing to find out about a fabric because it informs the pattern, cutting, sewing, and finishing, as well as the functionality of the design itself. Learn about each type of fabric before you so much as pick up a sewing machine. "The difference between wovens and knits is like a Tennessee walking horse and a thoroughbred racing horse," says Cecilia Metheny, professor at Parsons The New School for Design and a frequent presence at Mood. "The same pattern made in a woven or a knit will act very differently." (Read on for more information about the third, miscellaneous category, nonwovens.)

WOVEN FABRICS

Wovens are formed via weaving: Threads interlaced on a loom form a crisscrossing

pattern. Think of the structure of the fabric as a grid. Classic cotton shirting, denim, and silk crepe are some typical woven fabrics.

CUTTING AGAINST THE GRAIN. Pattern pieces are typically laid out for cutting with their printed grainline exactly parallel to the selvage; this ensures that the garment hangs properly when worn. However, there are exceptions to the rule. Garments **cut on the bias** are arranged with pattern grainlines at a 45-degree angle; this creates extra drape or a body-skim ming effect in the finished garment. (**Bias tape** is a thin strip of fabric cut on the bias that's used to cover raw seam

Above: Fabrics with detailing along the selvages, like this printed dress from Donna Karan's spring/summer 2014 collection, lend themselves to a cross-grain layout.

Previous pages: Bolts and swatches of specialty fabric at Mood's NYC store.

36/ THE MOOD GUIDE TO FABRIC AND FASHION

A SENSE OF DIRECTION

The lengthwise yarns—those that run parallel to the fabric's finished edge in woven fabrics—are called the WARP; the yarns that run perpendicular to the warp are called the WEFT.

The GRAIN LINES refer to the direction of the warp and weft. These should be identified for each woven fabric you plan to work with. The grain that's parallel to the warp is called the STRAIGHT GRAIN; the weft direction is often referred to as the CROSS-GRAIN. When you make a purchase, the salesperson cuts or tears the fabric on the cross-grain.

The self-finished edges along the sides of a roll are called the SELVAGE of that fabric. The selvage is a key navigational line when you're cutting a pattern: It runs parallel to the warp.

> **"I never came across any fabric that disobeyed me."**
>
> —MADELEINE VIONNET

Above: A look from Rick Owens's fall/winter 2002 collection. Jersey fabrics aren't just for athletic wear.

edges; because it's cut on the bias, it follows curves smoothly.)

Sometimes a pattern piece is laid out and cut on the **cross-grain**: the direction perpendicular to the selvage. Fabrics with detailing along the selvages lend themselves to a cross-grain layout, which places a border print or embellishment feature along the hemline or other horizontal garment section. Pieces cut this way might be a bit less stable, so it's important to consider the potential effect on the finished garment. Certain fabrics, such as silk charmeuse, can be cut a few degrees **off-grain** for better sewing results. For the best results, beginners should generally plan on following a pattern's layout diagram.

KNIT FABRICS

Knits include T-shirt jersey, spandex, and sweatshirt terry; they are constructed by **looping** yarns together. Due to their structure, knits always stretch to some degree, though some stretch more—a great deal more—than others (see Stretch Fabrics on page 38). As a general rule, they tend to be more challenging to sew than wovens. A machine called a

serger (or **overlocker**) is recommended for the most professional results; a **coverstitch/ chainstitch machine** is used in manufacturing to finish knit-fabric hems. Without these, it's possible to sew knits using a **stretch** or **zigzag stitch** on a conventional machine, though for a professional-grade finish, this shortcut won't cut it.

NONWOVENS

Nonwovens, also referred to in the industry as **other fabric types**, comprise any fabric formed directly from fibers or from non-fiber sources without weaving or knitting. A prime example is felt, in which wool or synthetic

The front, or outside, of the fabric is known as the face or right side; the back is also known as the wrong side, and, in theory at least, not meant to be seen. On a roll or bolt, the face of the fabric is usually on the outside. On a swatch, it might not be possible to tell the difference (which is why the face of a swatch should be marked before you leave the store). Of course, many designers delight in using the wrong side of fabric on the outside of a garment, and you can, too: The shiny face of silk charmeuse can feel extra-smooth against the skin and provide a matte look for the exterior, while a reversed faux-shearling creates a cuddly look on a jacket's collar.

Fabrics explicitly designed to be visible on both sides are double-faced. When double-faced fabrics are made of two layers attached together, such as double-faced wool coating, the fabric layers can be pulled apart at the raw edge of a garment so the hems can be finished cleanly on both sides.

fibers are compressed into a sheet of fabric using heat, pressure, and sometimes steam. Leather and faux leather, latex, foam, some interfacings (supplementary fabrics used to stabilize high-stress areas such as collars and plackets), and interlinings also fall into this category, as do (for example's sake) Swiffer cloths and paper. For the purposes of sewing, keep in mind that nonwovens can behave like wovens or like knits. Leathers, foams, and felt don't stretch; rubber might. Test the fabric with your hands to get a sense of how it will sew up. Interfacings can be stretch or non-stretch, and should be paired with knit or woven fabric accordingly.

Sometimes, as with neoprene, a nonwoven element is **bonded** to a woven or knit element—that is, fused together with heat or an adhesive. These high-tech hybrids have the structure and futuristic appeal of a nonwoven on one side, and the more tactile softness of a traditional fabric on the other.

STRETCH FABRICS

Some woven fabrics stretch due to the inclusion of spandex fibers in the yarn. The easiest way to tell is, of course, to pull at the fabric. While all knit fabrics have some stretch built in structurally, some (such as body-hugging jerseys) also have additional spandex content for added comfort, recovery, or compression. And some (such as stiffer cotton jersey used for boxy or structured styles) aren't really meant to be pulled and tugged, and will get bent out of shape if this happens.

Most stretch fabrics stretch in one direc-

Above: A neoprene dress on the Balenciaga runway.

In calculating how much fabric to buy for a specific style, it's common to round up by about 20%. Every designer—even the world-famous ones—orders extra fabric to account for margin of error; this is the very reason Mood ends up with a trove of leftover designer fabrics each season!

STOCK CHECK
Another important question to ask the store: How much of the fabric is in stock? If you're planning to produce any sort of multi-piece collection—or if a fabric you love and plan to use again someday is in short supply—it can make sense to buy more than you need for a single garment, if the budget allows.

A blouse might require only two yards of silk, but if you might want to use it for a dress or two, too—or simply to stock your sewing room—it could make sense to go the whole nine yards, as it were.

tion: in the cross-grain direction. However, some fabrics—notably those used for activewear and swimwear, as well as some stretch denims—offer **two-way stretch** (sometimes, confusingly, called **four-way stretch**), which enables them to stretch and recover in all directions. This bilateral stretch, as well as the addition of synthetic stretch fibers, also aids in **recovery**—that is, how well the fabric returns to size and shape once it's been stretched. (Good recovery from two-way stretch prevents baggy-kneed skinny jeans, say, or distended bikini bottoms.) Ask a salesperson if you're not sure about the stretch properties of a particular fabric.

YARDAGE REQUIREMENT
Once you've found a fabric you'd like to use, the next question is: How much of it to buy? If you have a commercial pattern, it should list a yardage requirement for all textiles needed (fashion fabric, lining, and interfacing) for various widths of fabric and for each size of garment included in the pattern. If you're not working with a commercial pattern, consult an existing pattern with a similar style and silhouette; Mood and many stores keep a library of patterns on file.

The fabric's **width** must also be considered. A wider fabric usually results in a smaller fabric requirement, and vice versa. The more pattern pieces that can be cut on a width of fabric, the shorter the length of that fabric you'll need. It's all about total surface area: A wide, short rectangle can have the same area as a longer, narrower one. However, some designs—those with extra-long or –wide garment sections, or with pieces cut on the bias—fit better on wider or longer fabric. If in doubt, do a test layout on a gridded mat or the floor to see how much fabric your pattern really needs.

SHRINKAGE AND CARE
Many, but not all, fabrics in a fabric store come pretreated and washed. If a fabric isn't preshrunk when it's sold on the roll, it will need to be treated before cutting and sewing, so ask a salesperson. (This often applies to "raw" fabrics, like natural cotton and indigo denim that have been only minimally processed after weaving.) Shrinkage also increases the amount of yardage you need for your project, so ask if the salesperson can estimate a percentage of shrinkage. If preshrinking is required, wash or clean and then iron or steam the yardage according to care instructions—again, ask the salesperson to be sure!—before cutting.

"An all-around tip for working with any fabric is to truly listen to what it's telling you to do. Fabric has a silent voice, but in time you will be able to hear what it's saying, from which way to press a seam to which areas of the body it will work best on."

—JOSHUA MCKINLEY, *PROJECT RUNWAY* SEASON 9 AND SEASON 2 ALL-STARS

ONE DIRECTION: ONE-WAY FABRICS

When a fabric has a non-symmetrical print or **nap** (raised surface)—such as a print whose motifs all have a distinct top or bottom, or a mohair texture that leans to one side—it's likely what's known as a **one-way fabric**. In this case, pattern pieces must be laid out in one direction to avoid coloration mismatches or motifs turned upside down; this is commonly referred to as a "with-nap" layout. (Imagine a velvet coat with one panel taking on a slightly different tone, say, or a flamingo-print shirt in which the flamingos face the wrong way on one sleeve). The special cutting requirements of a one-way fabric can increase the yardage requirements, often significantly. Ask a salesperson to help you calculate this if you're not sure.

Some fabrics require a single-layer layout in order to engineer perfect matches of prints or patterns along key seamlines. These include plaids, some stripes, large prints, and embellished or special-occasion fabrics like lace or embroidered textiles. The larger the repeat (size of, or spacing between, individual motifs), the more fabric needed to ensure a pleasingly matched layout.

LINER NOTES

While fashion fabric is what gives a garment its immediate appeal, there are often hidden layers inside it that make it comfortable, long-lasting, and flattering.

Linings add warmth or comfort to fabrics. They also make it much easier to create a clean finish on the inside of a garment (such

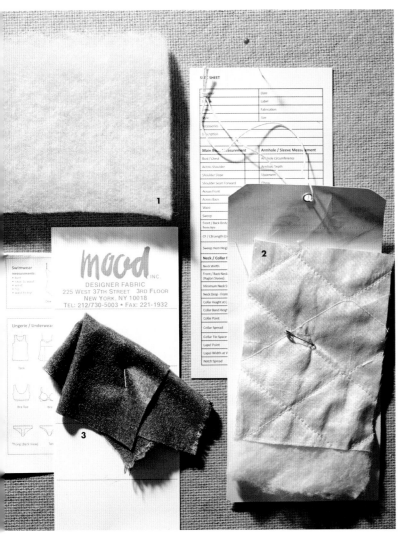

as a blazer, which would otherwise require extensive bias-tape finishing on its seam allowances). Structured garments, with foundation layers of interfacing or under-lining (see page 44), boning, or padding, benefit from a lining that both conceals and protects all the inner workings. Does your style require a lining? Silk habutai (also known as China silk) and the cellulose-based cupro (short for cuprammonium rayon, and also sometimes called by the trade name Bemberg) are two popular lining choices. Be sure to choose something with a slippery feel for ease of entry.

Interfacings provide garments with an invisible support system. These fabrics are used to stabilize fabrics that are difficult to sew and strengthen high-stress areas such as pockets, cuffs, and plackets. As a general rule, anything with buttons or tailoring (shirting, pants, suiting) requires some interfacing. Some styles are fusible and bond to the fabric with heat. The weight and style of an interfacing or interlining must be appropriate for the fabric itself; a too-heavy interfacing might show through a sheer fabric, while fusible might cause puckering on a delicate silk.

Interfacing comes in a wide variety of types: woven, knit, a hybrid called weft-insertion, nonwoven, hair canvas, and more. There are also many weights to choose from. Ask a salesperson to recommend a good match for your fashion fabric.

Interlinings are generally used between

Opposite:
1. Woven fusible interfacing
2. Woven fusible interfacing
3. Nonwoven fusible tricot knit interfacing
4. Nonwoven sew-in interfacing
5. Nonwoven fusible interfacing
6. Sew-in hymo/hair canvas

Above:
1. Cotton batting
2. Prequilted interlining
3. Wool flannel

When you shop for fabric, ask yourself— or the sales staff— these questions, so you have all the information you need to determine whether the textile you love is suitable for your intended project.

- What is the fiber composition?

- Is it a woven, knit, or neither?

- What is the width?

- What is the straight grain? Which is the cross-grain? How do the selvages look?

- Which is the right side and which is the wrong side? Can the fabric be reversed if desired?

- Is it stretch or non-stretch? In which direction(s)? What is the percentage of stretch?

- Is it a one-way fabric?

- Is the fabric pre-shrunk? If not, how much shrinkage can you expect?

- What is the estimated yardage needed for the garment? How does the width affect this?

- Special yardage requirements: Cutting on the bias? One-way fabric?

- How much of the fabric is in stock?

- How much does it make sense to buy?

- Does it need lining and/or interfacing?

- What notions and trims will be needed to make the desired style?

- What are the care instructions for the fabric?

layers of a garment, such as a coat, to add warmth or bulk. Quilting, batting, flannel, or windproof high-tech fabrics serve this purpose. (Note that "interlining" is sometimes used as a synonym for "underlining" [see below]. We use it here to denote fabrics intended to provide insulation.)

Underlinings or **backings** are a second, hidden layer that can be added just beneath the fashion fabric. Typical fabrics used for underlining are silk organza, organdy, cotton batiste, cotton flannelette, or muslin. The underlining is cut exactly the same size and shape as the fashion fabric pieces, basted to them on the wrong side, and then the two layers are treated as one throughout construction. Underlining is an essential part of many couture sewing techniques, as it provides light structure, opacity, and a layer you can mark and hand-sew hems and edges to, so stitching doesn't show on the garment's right side.

EXTRA CREDIT: NOTIONS AND TRIMS

Mood and many other fabric outlets sell more than fabric: Sections dedicated to notions and trims make for one-stop sewing-room shopping. Yet many people who come in— even brilliant fashion students—don't know the difference between the two.

Notions are sewing accessories with a functional purpose, the nuts and bolts of a sewing kit: thread, zippers, snaps, seam rippers, chalk, hook-and-eye closures, pins, needles, tape measures, and the like. Of course, designers can and do use notions as

Opposite: Underlinings (clockwise from top left):

White organza
White cotton batiste
Green flannelette

Opposite and above:
Notions and trims, such as zippers (left) and fringe (above), can serve function or fashion (or both).

in general, the following rules will help you treat fine fabric with finesse.

- Prepare fabric as needed before cutting and sewing—this means preshrinking cottons and some wools in the wash, or steam-shrinking some silks and wools with a steam iron or steamer. Press or steam the fabric before laying out and cutting pattern pieces to ensure a quality result.

- Work with weights. When laying out and cutting fabric, avoid using pins anywhere but between pattern pieces or, if necessary, in the seam allowances, especially with fine wovens or knits, as they might leave holes in the material.

- Run thread through beeswax before hand-sewing with it to make it more resilient. Wax prevents the thread from tangling as you stitch, and helps the garment to hold up better over time. Some threads are available prewaxed; consider buying this type of thread to save time.

- Basting seam allowances together before permanently sewing seams lessens the stress placed on the body of fabric as it moves through the machine.

design elements (as in exposed zippers or contrast-color thread).

Trims are decorative elements that add visual interest to a garment: buttons, piping, rickrack, ribbon, ruffles, and lace edgings.

HANDLE WITH CARE

There's no point in buying fine fabric if you plan on leaving it crumpled on the floor like pajamas. Fabric should be stored and sewn properly to yield the best results for your design. The individual fabric chapters that follow provide fabric-specific pointers, but

PHIL SAUMA ON HOW TO SPOT GOOD FABRIC

The majority of the fabric at Mood comes from somewhat more modest origins: designers' sample rooms and showrooms; mills and their warehouses; the shelves of factories in the Garment District and overseas. But who selects it all, separating the good from the bad, the wheat from the chaff?

Phil Sauma. Since joining the family business, he has made daily purchases ranging from one roll to thousands at a time—directly from manufacturers, designers' sample rooms, fabric mills and converters, and garment factories. Some is produced expressly for Mood or already in stock; most of it, however, is left over from designers' collections. Every bolt that makes its way to Mood's shelves must first meet Phil's exacting requirements—that is, unless it has otherwise been vetted by the world's top designers. "They are buying from the best mills in the world, and it has to meet their standards, so the dirty work is done for me," says Phil.

When that's not the case, however, Phil's eagle eyes and sensitive hands take over. "Factories cut all levels of stuff, good and bad," he says. "It's my job to be able to differentiate and buy the right items—fabric that offers good quality at the right price so I can sell it at a fair price. I don't think any of our customers come to get a bargain-basement price, but they don't want to get ripped off."

That may be a good general guideline for shopping—as Phil puts it, "you get what you pay for"—but that's not to say that less expensive fabric, as a category, is always less desirable. The cost of raw materials plays a part, too. Cotton gauze will always be cheaper than cashmere coating, but both are beautiful and appropriate for different types of designs. And while the Mood team generally favors natural fibers over cheap substitutes, synthetic doesn't have to be a dirty word. Futurist designers like Yohji Yamamoto

make heavy use of polyester and nylon on the runways; new technology means that these fabrics can be just as soft as, and even more uniquely textured than, silk—at a far gentler price (and without the dry-cleaning bills). The finest Japanese novelty synthetics actually cost more than some silks! And sometimes, the very presence of synthetic fiber is what makes a design possible. If you plan to pleat fabric at home, for example, "you have to have some synthetic content, or the fabric won't hold the pleat," says Phil.

WHY IS QUALITY SO IMPORTANT?

Better quality fabric at any price point lasts longer and looks and wears better. How, then, to determine whether a fabric has bang for the buck? It's an elusive proposition, but the best strategy is to familiarize yourself with fabrics of all types and comparison shop.

Ultimately, there's also the cost of your own time to consider, Phil points out. "If you're taking the time and effort to make it yourself, there's something to be said for not scrimping on fabric," he says. "If you're going to make a meal yourself, don't you want the best ingredients?"

PHIL SAUMA'S SHOPPING RULES

These principles are the same ones Phil relies on when buying fabric for Mood. Use them to ensure that you choose the best quality textiles for your garment.

SEE IT, FEEL IT, TOUCH IT, DRAPE IT. Though Phil credits his own sixth sense for evaluating fabric to "years of experience," he maintains

ERRICK PERRYMAN

Fabric Cutter, Wool
and Fourth Floor
Fabrics, Mood NYC

Hometown:
Chicago, Illinois

Favorite fabric:
"Cashmere knit—
it has a very rich
feeling to it."

"If I didn't have some kind of design perspective, I don't think I would be able to do this job," Errick says. He began working at Mood in 2006. He moved to New York from Chicago after graduating from the Illinois Institute of Art where he studied fashion design. "I got hired right on the spot because I had a background of working with fabrics in Chicago."

Mixing new fabrics with old ones, pulling fabrics, rotating them, and putting them on display for customers all help Errick with his own design process.

"Often when I drape something for the store I get an idea for a concept I want to try at home. Draping is a form of drawing for me." He loves working with knits most. And he favors clothing with a creative edge that is still chic and sophisticated.

Errick says he's learned a lot both creatively and practically from working at Mood. "I interact with so many different personalities here. I've learned to listen more closely to the customer. I need to be alert so I can understand what people are looking for."

Above: Silk jersey dresses draped by Errick Perryman.

that many times, simple instinct is the best way to determine a fabric's value. "There's just a certain hand to good fabric; it either has it or it doesn't," he says. In other words, make sure you like the look, the texture, and the way it moves. Many good fabrics simply exude an air of quality. Visit high-end clothing and fabric stores, even if you're not buying, and study the drape and hand of fine fabrics (and cheap ones) to familiarize yourself with the difference. Explore the way they feel, the way they hang, the way they look in the light. Over time, you'll develop an eye and a hand for distinguishing fine from mediocre textiles.

WATCH YOUR WEIGHTS. Does the weight of the fabric make sense for the design of the garment? This topic is covered in more depth in Chapter 4, but its importance can't be overstated. Mood carries a range of fabric weights, selected by Phil with functionality in mind. "A lot of silhouettes, especially suits or pants, require a certain amount of weight to the fabric," says Phil. "Sometimes, silk has to have a certain weight to fall right. On the other hand, with certain styles, like blouses, the fabric can't be too heavy. Weight has a lot to do with results." If you're working from a pattern, it should provide information about what kind of fabric to use. Discuss with a salesperson if you aren't sure how well a fabric will work for a particular style.

INSPECT THE ROLL FOR COLOR. Believe it or not, solid colors aren't always so solid. "Sometimes a roll of fabric has spots, or is shaded in certain parts," Phil warns. "Or the top of a roll will be lighter and the bottom will be darker. Cheap dyeing looks like that. And if you sew with fabric that isn't properly dyed, it affects the garment. The sleeve won't match the front, for example, and they will look like two different colors." Examine the roll or bolt as the salesperson unrolls it, and don't let him or her cut until you've made sure the color is uniform.

READ THE FINE PRINTS. "Bad printing bleeds," says Phil. "And I've seen lots of two-color prints where the placement is off and the fill color has been printed off the outline." Needless to say, neither of these is a good thing. If buying a printed fabric, inspect it during unrolling for any out-of-line placement or blurred edges.

IF THE FABRIC IS KNIT OR HAS A NAP, TEST FOR PILLING. Fabrics that pill are a real pill. Friction can cause fibers to become dislodged from the fabric's yarn and cluster together above the surface, creating unsightly nubbins and weakening the fabric in the process. "My rule of thumb is to rub the fabric in a circular motion 20 times and see what happens," says Phil. "If you start to see fibers coming up or light pilling, it's going to pill." It's true that the occasional fabric will have been designed with a pilled surface—Alexander Wang is one designer who uses such fabrics to unique effect in T-shirts and coats—but there's a big difference between a uniformly textured designer fabric that keeps its look and having the rear of your stretch pants fuzz up and disintegrate.

SCRATCHY? SCRATCH IT. "A wool that's not finished correctly will feel like a piece of sandpaper," says Phil. "You definitely don't want that." There's one exception to this rule: Some heritage wools, like Harris Tweed, are naturally unfinished, but they also have a thick, robust texture that makes them look expensive. How to know the difference between quality and inferior fabric by texture? Use your instincts. Feel the fabric in your hands, and fold and crunch it; hold it up to your cheek or the inside of your forearm, or another sensitive area of the body. If your gut reaction is that you don't like it, move on.

WHEN IN DOUBT, GO ITALIAN. The same principle that (for most people) applies to food also applies to fabric. "If it's made from start to finish in Italy, generally they do really nice things," says Phil. "The yarn is great. The weaving is great. The finishing is amazing."

LAST WORD: LOOK FOR THE SIGNS!

At Mood as in many other fabric stores, each section is clearly marked with an overhead sign indicating the type of fabric stocked there. Sometimes shelves are arranged by fiber (such as Silk), other times by category (e.g., Swimwear Fabric). It sounds so simple, but many a frantic query could be avoided if customers simply read the signs in the store. Where's the tulle section? Ah, I'm in the tulle section!

> **"I work directly with the cloth the way blowers work the hot glass. It must be done fast and instinctively, letting gravity do most of the work to really get the most out of the material."**
>
> —ISABEL TOLEDO

If you want to behold the beauty of Italian fabric firsthand, a good place to start is on the via della Spiga in Milan, the capital of Italy's storied fashion industry. This narrow cobblestone street is a shopping mecca to rival any in the world, and its boutiques are stocked with runway-fresh finery. Prada. Dolce & Gabbana. Bottega Veneta. Buttery cashmere. Specially textured silk. Luxury leather. The fashion is glorious—and priced accordingly.

Yet even more exclusive than these luxury storefronts is a showroom located around the corner on via Gesù, behind an unmarked door and up a flight of marble stairs. Even most Italian designers don't get an invitation to come up here—but Phil Sauma does. This is Gandini Tessuti Alta Moda—Italian for High Fashion Textiles, though something ineffably glamorous is lost in the translation. Entering through a hand-carved mahogany doorway, visitors greet the proprietress, Susy Gandini. This is no ordinary office: think rare antiques, herringbone parquet floors, even a bell whose provenance is the Eiffel Tower. And Susy herself is no ordinary textile dealer. "She's like Sophia Loren," says Phil. "The most elegant Italian lady you can imagine, decked out in pearl necklaces and couture, fluent in four or five languages. My wife says that Susy is who she wants to be in 30 years. What I love about her is she's a freak for Ferraris. She drives a red one."

Susy is also a freak for fabrics, and has run Gandini—founded in 1925 by her husband's father—since 1961. Gandini creates luxury fabrics of sumptuous texture, detail, and hand feel: lavish bouclés, high-tech brocades. And she sells them to the best of the best: Chanel, Valentino, Armani, Dior. Susy herself is a key player in fashion history: Yves Saint Laurent and Christian Dior were dear friends as well as clients. That type of relationship tends to be the case at Gandini. "She has maybe 15 customers in the world," says Phil. "When you come in, it's ten minutes of business and two hours of chatting."

Gandini is what's known as a converter. Converters buy and customize raw fabric—known to the trade as greige goods—from mills, which are the manufacturers that use looms and knitting machines to weave or knit yarn into fabric. The role of the converter is often a creative one; the finishing of a fabric, which can include special washes and textures, dyeing, and other surface treatments, can have as much to do with how a fabric looks and behaves as the fiber and construction itself. In Gandini's case, the mills she works with are mostly centuries-old family businesses nestled in the spectacular hills above Lake Como. Susy collaborates with the mills to design and produce seasonal collections, which she then presents under her name to her roster of elite clients; to keep the designers happy and their runway shows distinctive, only one fashion house is allowed to purchase each fabric.

Fortunately for the rest of the world, some of these fabrics—test runs, sample yardage, and the like—end up at Mood. Each year, Phil buys small amounts, one roll at a time, for the New York store. Susy's associates carefully unfurl each roll and measure it for him, meter after meter, by hand (a practice unheard-of at modern mills and converters, which check the yardage of a purchase by machine). That anyone who happens to be in New York City can walk in off the street and see and feel (and even buy) Gandini's specialty silks, wools, and bouclés is something of a fashion miracle. However, with prices tending to hit the triple digits for a yard, it's not for everyone—even ambitious Parsons students. "Usually, we sell to a lot of high-end custom clients," says Phil. "There's one designer in particular from D.C. and Palm Beach who buys a lot of Gandini to make suits and dresses for events for society women. The fabric has some glitz and glamour to it. Most kids wouldn't even know what to make with it."

Fabric and Design

It's easy to be overcome with inspiration when flitting about the fabric store, but sewing is equal parts art and science. No matter how beautiful the material, if it doesn't serve the function of the intended garment, the design will be an unwearable flop. That means that when it comes to choosing the fabric for your pattern—or choosing a pattern for your fabric, as the case may be—education is as important as inspiration.

So which comes first, the fabric or the pattern? Should you take a pattern into the fabric store, or buy fabric first and then decide what to make? Most fashion designers feel it's a chicken-or-egg question. "I love shopping for fabric first because the fabric guides me and provides the necessary inspiration to make a garment an absolute masterpiece," says *Project Runway* Season 7 alumnus Anthony Williams. "On the other hand, when I start with a pattern and then choose the fabric, I find myself in control and very committed to ensuring my initial vision, by hook or by crook."

This chapter addresses both sides of the equation: how to select the best fabric for your design, as well as some creative ways to design with fabric you simply can't resist.

FUNCTION AND FABRIC: CHOOSING THE RIGHT MATERIAL FOR YOUR PATTERN

These tips are worth keeping in mind when you're deciding how to fabricate your design (or how to design around your fabric, if that's the way you're working).

CONSIDER WEIGHT. A fabric's **weight** significantly affects how it will behave—and how it will look when sewn into any given pattern. In general, lighter weights correspond to warmer weather and vice versa, but there are always exceptions (a heavy linen would make a great spring jacket, while a fine wool crepe would work well as a winter blouse). As for sewing and construction, it simply might not make sense to use some fabric weights for some styles. A fragile gauze can't support the weight or stress of snaps or Velcro, even if you add interfacing. Chunky zippers tend to create rippling bulges when added to lightweight silk jackets. On the other end of the weight spectrum, a faux-fur T-shirt might sound cool, but in reality would be very hot (yet not practical enough to function as outerwear). Yet sometimes—barring functionality issues, of course—it's fun to fabricate a pattern in a totally unexpected fabric weight: an anorak in featherweight faux silk, say, or a structured neoprene T-shirt (see So Wrong It's Right on page 60 for more ideas).

CONSIDER DRAPE. Different fabrics hang differently on the body due to properties of different fibers as well as the fabric's weave, weight, and finishing treatment. Not all fabrics made from the same fiber behave the same way. Fabrics that **drape** well, or are **drapey**—that hang and move in a fluid,

"When I was four years old, I was already talking about becoming a designer.... I always had it in mind that a designer had beautiful fabrics around her, and a big sketchbook, and would drape cloth around a mannequin, and go out to lunch. It seemed like a very glamorous life."

—ANNA SUI

Previous pages: Fabric influences the result of a design through color, texture, function, and drape. Clockwise from top left: A mannequin at Mood demonstrates the sculptural quality of silk gazar; part of Mood's selection of silks; an Elsa Schiaparelli creation contrasts her signature color, shocking pink, with black as shown in *Vogue*, April, 1951; fashion illustrator Esta Nesbitt's mixed-media take on feathers and fringe offers design inspiration.

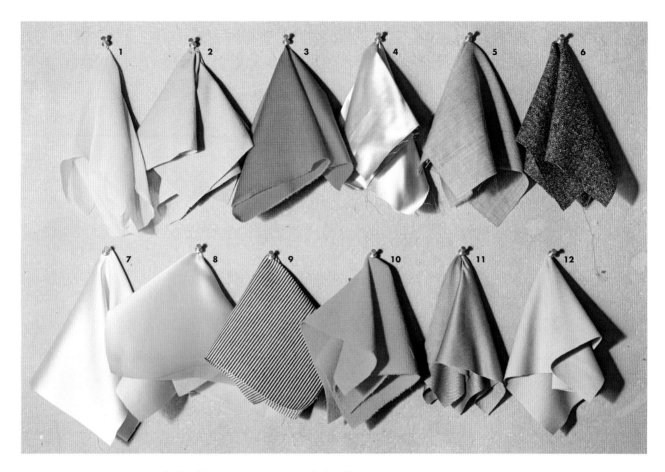

Above: Variation in drape
1. Chiffon
2. Broadcloth
3. Sateen
4. Duchesse satin
5. Tropical wool suiting
6. Donegal wool tweed
7. Silk charmeuse
8. Silk organza
9. Denim
10. Wool crepe
11. Silk jersey
12. Ponte di roma

body-skimming manner—include silk crepe de chine (a.k.a. CDC) and charmeuse. Generally, if you're making a flowing evening dress or a pair of billowing trousers, or anything with an extravagant degree of volume, this will be a good thing.

The opposite of this is a fabric that has **structure or body**, which is another way of saying "stiffness." Patterns with a silhouette that is intended to stand away from the underlying body, and those that are closely fitted, call for a certain degree of structure or bounce: most coats and structured jackets, '60s-style shift or sheath dresses, and snugly fitting pants and skirts. An A-line silhouette

rendered in silk crepe would simply look saggy, whereas a sturdy wool really brings out the shape.

Examples of textiles with body include silk taffeta and organza, which create lightweight volume and expansiveness for dramatic and dressy looks. Some fabrics—certain types of cupro come to mind—might look and feel like they should be drapey, but when made into a garment have a bouncy, away-from-the-body quality. To determine a fabric's drape, "try it on" in the mirror: Hang it against the body and see how it moves. Does it collapse against the form, billow away from it, or remain stiff and structured? This

///

JUAN CARLOS
RIOS NEGRON

Salesperson and
Master Draper,
Mood NYC

Hometown:
San Juan, Puerto Rico

Favorite fabric:
"Heavy satin or bro-
cade. They're more
sculptural and allow
you to take an archi-
tectural approach."

///

Though Mood's New York shelves brim with beautiful fabric, what really brings the merch to life is the store's famous mannequins, which sport elabo- rately draped swaths of material that look like couture creations. The brain behind many of them is J.C., a student at the Fashion Institute of Technology and aspiring fashion designer who moon- lights on Mood's sales staff. When he's not helping customers, he's dreaming up designs in real time, sculpting silk or cotton into intri- cate shapes using only pins, scissors, and his imagination.

Fashion of the high- drama variety has always called to J.C.: "When I was five, I'd make my mother get into her wed- ding gown at 6 a.m. because I wanted to recreate a scene from *Beauty and the Beast*," he says. In college in San Juan, he studied sculpture and worked in the stu- dent theater's costume atelier. In 2011, he arrived in New York to pursue a second bachelor's degree in fashion and quickly became acquainted with Mood through his class assignments. His frequent shopping trips led him to apply for a job, and he was soon getting hands-on with the fabric. "I really enjoy working in 3-D," he says. "I discover more things that way." His designs were a hit with customers, and the mannequins mul- tiplied throughout the store. Now, they change with the sea- sons, offering customers inspiration they can reach out and touch. "It really gives a taste of what the fabric can do," J.C. says of his dress-form design oeuvre. "It's not the same as seeing it on a bolt."

will give a hint as to how it will behave. Can you fold it easily? If not, don't use it for an intricately pleated gown. Is it transparent? Then it won't make a warm winter coat. Common sense is your best weapon against an unsuccessful design—so think twice before you cut once.

CONSIDER BUDGET. How much can you afford? Do you need to spend a fortune on a French bouclé, or would a simple, solid-colored material suffice for your design? Is the fabric secondary to the shape? Is there an affordable substitute for what you might be looking for—for example, could a nice-quality wool flannel stand in for cashmere? "Some of the new synthetic silks are beautiful, and they're four dollars a yard," says Tim Gunn. "And you can barely tell the difference."

CONSIDER YOUR SKILL LEVEL. No matter the price—but especially if the price is high—your sewing abilities should also play a role in making the decision about a fabric. As a general rule of thumb, more difficult fabrics are slippery or stretchy, or tissue-thin. Heavier fabrics require special needles, but are otherwise more likely to stay in place. When in doubt, cotton wovens are an easy place to start. "Make sure you know how to handle it," says Parsons' Cecilia Metheny. "Don't buy a 90-dollar-a-yard fabric because you're madly in love with it and then destroy it. You need to know how to construct with it."

BEGINNER

Cotton shirting and other cotton and
    cotton-blend wovens

Linen wovens

Most wool wovens, except for gauze

Bonded fabrics

Felt and fleece

INTERMEDIATE

Jersey and stretch fabrics (cotton, rayon)

Silk (medium weight and wovens with body)

Denim (denim needle required)

Fine voiles and challis

Faux leather

ADVANCED

Silk jersey

Lightweight silk (chiffon, gauze, charmeuse)

Silk brocade

Lace, sequined, and beaded fabrics

Fur and faux fur

Leather

YOUR CLOSET IS YOUR "COLLECTION." Before designers buy fabric for a collection, they cut (or order) swatches from various sources and arrange and rearrange them, often alongside sketches and inspiration images, to determine the final assortment. Whether you're making a garment at home to fill a void in your wardrobe or creating a multi-piece runway presentation, consider the balance among the different fabrics and textures.

Before you shop for fabric, look at what you have and ask the questions the pros ask themselves. Is there enough variety in weight, from heavier to lighter? Do the colors you have tell the story you want to tell? (**Color story** is a popular industry term.) Is the overall effect too dark or dull, and would the addition of one bright color (in fashionista-

> "For me, the idea of a dress is mental. I conceive it and create it by dreaming. And finally, after searching, I end up holding it in my hands."
>
> —MADELEINE VIONNET

With elements of a garment that aren't load bearing—a collar, say, or a sheer ruffle overlay—it's **okay to layer light over heavy**. Generally speaking, the lightest material should not carry the weight or stress of anything heavier. It would be okay to have sheer chiffon sleeves attached to a thicker, stiffer bodice, but not to have a sheer chiffon bodice holding heavy sleeves in place.

GETTING CREATIVE: UNEXPECTED WAYS TO FABRICATE YOUR DESIGN

Though it's important to keep your garment's functional requirements in mind when choosing fabric, that doesn't mean you have to use exactly what the pattern tells you to, or to follow your first fabric instinct. Sometimes breaking with tradition—or combining different fabrics in one garment—is what makes a design interesting and original. Here are a few suggestions for how to think outside the (basic) bolt.

LAYER UP. "Layering a sheer fabric over a print creates movement and dimension," says Denis Grams, manager of the silk section at Mood in New York. "This works beautifully with silks." A brightly colored lining for a sheer dress (instead of the predictable flesh tone or black) can be fresh and unexpected. Even a simple slip-dress pattern can be transformed with this clever technique. Try layering sheer black over a pale color, a print on top of a print—the possibilities are limitless.

CREATIVE LINING. For lined styles where the lining will occasionally show—like suit jack-

Above: A look from *Project Runway* designer Sweet P's "Ghosts in the Garden" collection, which combined unexpected fabric textures and weights.

> "In my 'Ghosts in the Garden' collection, I paired silk chiffon with leather. I love the mix of the hard and the soft."
>
> —SWEET P, *PROJECT RUNWAY* SEASON 4 AND ALL-STAR

speak, the **pop color**) elevate the effect? A good wardrobe, like a good designer collection, has a balanced approach. "It's not really about combining as many unique fabrics together as I can just to serve the purpose of being 'unusual,'" says Joshua McKinley of *Project Runway* Season 9. "It's about making sure that I focus on the integration of textiles that can truly elevate the end result."

TEXTILES IN COMBINATION. When using more than one type of fabric within a single garment, in general **it's best to keep weights relatively evenly matched**, or at least to avoid weighing light down with heavy. If a drop-waist dress is diaphanous silk on the bodice and weighty wool in the skirt, the wool will tug the silk downward and tear

1. WHAT SEASON IS THE GARMENT FOR?
   If it's for spring or summer, look for a fabric that will feel good against skin. Cotton is a safe bet, and seek out lighter weights or cooler fabrics like linen or "tropical wool" (a summer-weight wool). For fall or winter, think warmth: wool, cashmere, heavy silks. All-season choices include mid-weight silks and cottons.

2. IS IT A TOP, BOTTOM, OR ALL-IN-ONE GARMENT?
   Look for top- or bottom-weight fabric if you need to.

3. SHOULD THE FABRIC BE LIGHT OR HEAVY?
   Will it need to support zippers, snaps, or other weighty closures, or is it meant to be ethereal and flowy? Is it outerwear or innerwear? Have a weight in mind.

4. DOES THE PATTERN CALL FOR A KNIT OR A WOVEN FABRIC?
   Most patterns require one or the other. Remember, knits will stretch and might not recover.

5. DOES THE DESIGN HUG THE BODY?
   If so, consider using a stretchy fabric. A stiff fabric, like denim, can compress and mold to the body because of its rigidity— good for jeans, not so good for a fitted tee.

6. SHOULD THE FABRIC BE FLUID, BOUNCY, OR STIFF?
   This depends on the design. Test the fabric with a mirror "try on."

7. DOES THE PATTERN HAVE A LOT OF FOLDS, GATHERING, OR RUCHING?
   If so, seek out a more fluid fabric and avoid anything too thick.

8. WHAT TYPES OF FABRIC ARE YOU COMFORTABLE SEWING?
   Consult page 57 for beginner, intermediate, and advanced options.

9. WHAT OTHER KINDS OF FABRICS DO YOU HAVE IN YOUR CLOSET (OR IN YOUR DESIGN COLLECTION)?
   Which fabrics might combine with what you have at home (or what you're planning to create) in an interesting way? Is there a great fabric you can use for more than one style? What is missing from your wardrobe?

10. DOES THE FABRIC FIT WITHIN YOUR BUDGET?
    How much fabric do you need for the pattern, and how much can you spend per yard?

ets or winter coats—consider using the lining as a design element of its own. An unexpected print or peek of vivid color can transform the feeling of a piece, functioning like a fun little secret you can share. "Some of our customers like to line their business suits with floral or paisley prints," says Tarek Mohammed, manager of the wool department in the New York store.

COLOR BLOCKING. A garment doesn't have to be made from just one fabric—even if its pattern calls for it. Try **color blocking** using a contrasting color or texture on the collar, sleeves, yoke, pockets, or placket (or all of the above). In fashion-production parlance, the secondary fabric is known as the **combo** (multiple variants are referred to as Combo 1, Combo 2, and so on). On a commercial pattern, this is usually called Contrast 1, 2, 3, etc. Different-colored panels can also be delineated with **style lines** rather than merely corresponding to functional pattern pieces.

One simple way to achieve this effect is to use the **wrong side** of the fabric on some garment elements. The effect can be beautifully subtle—or totally bold, if the wrong side is clearly discernible (as in, another color or texture) from the fabric's face.

PICKING UP THE PIECES. Scraps are more chic than they sound. **Appliqués**—essentially decorative cutout shapes affixed to a garment—are one interesting way to make use of scraps on the surface of a garment. Alabama Chanin makes use of both appliqué and reverse appliqué on her garments. The somewhat lost art of **quilting** or **patchworking**, while elaborate and time consuming, is a great way to use up extra fabric for a colorblocked look. Think beyond the typical Grandma's-bedspread shapes and colors and go for an interesting graphic effect. The quilts of Gee's Bend, made in the mid-1900s by a collective of women in Alabama and famously featured in an exhibition at the Whitney Museum, are a particularly inspiring example of the format.

SO WRONG, IT'S RIGHT. Sometimes, an audacious, unexpected fabric choice is the design.

Many avant-garde designers have built careers out of using the "wrong" fabric—or something that's not fabric at all—for an otherwise straightforward silhouette. "I always go to the interior fabrics section first, and I love using the wrong side of those heavy, textured jacquards," says Seth Aaron Henderson, *Project Runway* Season 7 winner. "I like to find something that not a lot of people would think of using." Martin Margiela created garments out of wigs, ski gloves, and, most famously, men's socks. Though it's not recommended to try this at home, designer Franc Fernandez made a dress for Lady Gaga out of meat! Tyvek, industrial felt, or even a shower curtain could be the basis for an amazing garment (or an interesting combo fabric or trim element).

GETTING INSPIRED

The most fun thing about fabric is the way it can single-handedly inform great design. Exploring texture, color, print, and drape firsthand at a fabric store (especially Mood) is a sure way to summon the muses, whether you're looking to make something with a pattern you have at home or planning to design a collection. "You have to play with the fabric," says Michael Costello from *Project Runway* Season 8. "When I go to Mood, I'll pull out a couple of yards and just touch and feel it. Then I'll run around the store with the bolt of fabric just to see the way it moves—and an idea will just hit me."

Another obvious, but essential, source of ideas is fashion itself. Magazines and blogs are great for gaining a sense of what's happening now, but it's also important to study fashion history. *Tim Gunn's Fashion Bible* (Gallery Books) is a great resource, as are

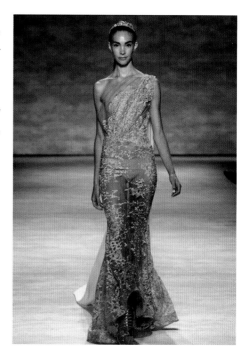

Above: A look by *Project Runway* Season 8 contestant Michael Costello utilizes sheer lace for dramatic effect. The way a fabric moves and feels can inspire a design.

> "If I'm inspired by a building, I'm not trying to make a dress that looks like the building. I'm going to make a dress that feels the way the building makes me feel."
>
> —SETH AARON HENDERSON, *PROJECT RUNWAY* SEASON 7 WINNER

> **"If I have done anything, it is to make ugly appealing. In fact, most of my work is concerned with destroying—or at least deconstructing—conventional ideas of beauty, of the generic appeal of the beautiful, glamorous, bourgeois woman."**
>
> —MIUCCIA PRADA

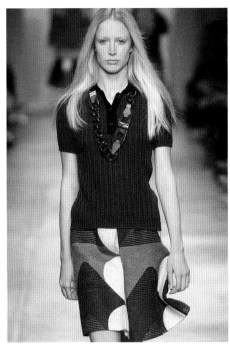

Above: Conflicting colors in Prada's spring/summer 2005 collection.

TAKE NOTE!

An idea is only good if you remember it in the first place. Most designers keep a notebook on hand at all times (and make use of their iPhone's Notes, Voice Memo, and camera functions). Mood sells and recommends the Fashionary series of sketchbooks, which have croquis forms (outlines of fashion figures, on which you can draw your original designs) and reference terms built right in. Pinterest and apps like Evernote have made collecting thoughts and ideas that much easier. Some designers, however, prefer more low-tech methods for keeping track of ideas: "I like to write or draw things on my hand so I won't forget them," says New York designer Mara Hoffman. Taking that idea one step further, Brazilian designer Alexandre Herchcovitch has a tattoo of a blank Post-it note on one hand.

The importance of good note-taking applies to fabric shopping, too. Using the shopping checklist on page 59, be sure to write down the relevant information about each fabric you swatch, and mark the face and wrong side, for future reference. When the time comes, you'll be prepared to make an informed decision about how much fabric to purchase and will know how much it will cost. After all, what good is a swatch if you have no idea what it is or where it came from?

the costume departments of museums and libraries (many of which have a robust online presence)—and, these days, Pinterest and Tumblr sites. The world is full of subcultures, past and present, with wildly original takes on dressing; one sure way to break out of a rut is to brush up on the fashion of Japanese Goth Lolitas, rockabillies, steampunks, and Teddy Boys. Traditional modes of dress, from the kimono to the sari, may not be fashion per se, but their colors, textures, and shapes have informed all of the greats. Learn about them, and they'll permeate your subconscious, inspiring form and function.

Of course, brilliant fashion ideas don't only arise out of other brilliant fashion ideas. (Alexander McQueen famously refused to look at his contemporaries' work for fear of contaminating his own vision.) In any case, be sure to visit art museums, travel, and study what others are wearing—even if you don't like what they're wearing.

Ideas can come from your immediate surroundings. Elsa Schiaparelli's signature shade of pink came into being when she couldn't stop staring at a friend's pink diamond ring. Karl Lagerfeld designed a collection inspired by his cat's eyes!

Good design ideas can often come from trying to make bad ideas better. Miuccia Prada and Marni are known for exploring "ugly" colors and prints; avant-garde knitwear designer Tom Scott once challenged himself to make a collection called "Things I Hate." A run-down part of town can abound with beautiful colors or textures. Michael Costello even based an entire collection around the shapes and color of the orange hazard fencing of a construction site. Sophie Buhai and Lisa Mayock of Vena Cava once garnered inspiration from the colors, textures, and hardware at Home Depot!

MOOD BOARDS. The **mood board** is a staple of the fashion design process—the closest thing to replicating what goes on in a designer's brain. It's a collage of fashion ideas, art and visual references, textile swatches, trims, and other imagery that informs the narrative of a collection, and assembling it is one of the most fun parts of the design process, whether you're an avid home sewer or an aspiring Karl Lagerfeld. Mood's own site has a host of them (naturally), while Pinterest has made designers' lives easier by making it possible to quickly cull images for mood boards from the internet (and other designers' and bloggers' Pinterest accounts). Some Tumblrs function as infinite mood boards as well. Of course, nothing replaces the tactile experience of a physical inspiration board in the design studio, with its physical fabric swatches that convey texture and drape, and hands-on editability. Create boards based on colors, cultural or historical themes, or to unite disparate ideas for sewing projects into one story that's uniquely yours.

"A piece of fabric can get me going."

—ANNA SUI

Here are some collected words of wisdom from the best in the business.

"Lots of designers have people do it for them, on the computer. But I do everything myself, and I like physically the work of sketching… Sometimes I have ideas before I wake up."

—KARL LAGERFELD

"I never look at other people's work. My mind has to be completely focused on my own illusions."

—ALEXANDER MCQUEEN

"I was never about dressing the person on the outside. I was always about dressing them on the inside."

—DONNA KARAN

"Design is an unknown. When I don't have any ideas I just pick up a piece of fabric and start working with it until something happens."

—GEOFFREY BEENE

I always want to have a new challenge involved. I need to put myself to the test, and if I make mistakes, it doesn't matter. What matters to me, instead, is making my dreams come true and putting them on display."

—YOHJI YAMAMOTO

"The way I approach each collection is exactly the same… the motivation has always been to create something new, something that didn't exist before."

—REI KAWAKUBO of Comme des Garçons

"I don't design clothes. I design dreams."

—RALPH LAUREN

"I'm not like most designers, who have to set sail on an exotic getaway to get inspired. Most of the time, it's on my walk to work, or sitting in the subway and seeing something random or out of context."

—ALEXANDER WANG

"To create something exceptional, your mindset must be relentlessly focused on the smallest detail."

—GIORGIO ARMANI

"Anything good ought to be copied and worn by many."

—COCO CHANEL

Cotton,
Linen, and Hemp

FROM ALL-AMERICAN blue-jeans denim to ultrafine shirting, cotton is the workhorse of our wardrobes. Its softness, ease, and versatility make it useful for every category in our closets; it can be warm or cool, soft or crisp, elegant or laid-back, delicate or durable. Cotton absorbs dyes easily, breaks in beautifully over time, and feels great against the skin in all climates. It's little wonder that it's the world's most popular fiber.

Cotton has been cultivated for clothing since the dawn of civilization, and much of human history has unfolded around its industry. (The most infamous example may be the United States Civil War, which arose in large part because of the demand of the cotton industry in the American South.) Today, the United States, China, and India are the largest producers of the fiber, but it's also grown around the world in places such as Australia, Brazil, Turkey, Pakistan, and Africa. It remains one of the most contentious crops in the world—cotton is an especially pesticide- and labor-intensive plant to grow—but fair-trade and organic cotton are growing in popularity and availability.

Cotton is a cellulose-based fiber that grows in a **boll,** or protective capsule, around the seeds of the mature cotton plant. Its structure, viewed in cross-section, looks like that of a collapsed tube or bean. Cellulose fibers have a number of appealing characteristics: they're soft, highly absorbent, and take dyes well. While most cultivated cotton is an off-white color, heirloom varieties can be green, tan, or reddish in tone. In recent years, cotton grown for these colors (known as **color-grown cotton**) has become more popular. Pima, Egyptian, and Sea Island cottons have a longer staple length (**staple** refers to the natural length of the fibers) and are thus softer and finer—and more expensive—than other varieties.

The cotton selection at Mood and other stores runs the gamut, but most popular is **shirting,** a category that encompasses woven cottons ideally suited for shirts. That doesn't mean they can't be used for other things, but be careful. Generally speaking, shirting fabrics are **top weights,** which means they're too sheer and not durable enough to be made into pants, fitted skirts, or other bottoms.

SEWING COTTON FABRICS

Woven fabrics made of cotton and its cousins (**linen** and **hemp,** which are also covered in this chapter) are often, but not always, easy to sew; beginners generally do well with them, and many of the problems associated with silks and knits (slipperiness, out-of-control fraying, stretching while sewing) don't apply to cotton wovens. The basic rules of sewing all fabrics apply to cottons—think twice before you cut once, and so on—but here are a few key factors to keep in mind.

THINK SHRINK. Cotton shrinks—a lot. Is your fabric preshrunk? Ask a salesperson to be sure. Even if it is, however, Mood recommends testing shrinkage first. Cut a 10" x 10" (25 cm x 25 cm) square of fabric, **label the length and width,** wash and dry it as you would the garment you'll be

> "I have an entire rack in my wardrobe devoted to shirts. A crisp white shirt looks good under anything and there are so many variations: French cuff, beaded collar, tunic, mandarin, tuxedo, piqué, swiss dot… I could never have too many."
>
> —JENNA LYONS,
> J. CREW CREATIVE
> DIRECTOR

making, and measure it again. If it shrinks, be sure to wash and preshrink large sheets of the fabric before cutting pattern pieces. (In the unlikely event that your cotton is dry-clean-only, steam-shrink the fabric instead—see the silks chapter, page 124, for more detailed instructions.)

CHOOSE THE RIGHT NEEDLE. Cotton comes in an immense variety of weights, and one needle size does not fit all. Universal needles in size 80/12, however, suit many cottons just fine. The most delicate voiles pair well with Microtex or sharp needles, while denim and heavy-duty duck and drill require designated denim needles, which are sharp and have a thicker shaft. If you'll be using thicker thread for topstitching on cotton outerwear, use a special topstitching needle.

PRESS HERE. As with all fabrics, cotton seams must be pressed for a professional look. In the case of cotton, which tends to crease easily, this is especially important (and luckily, not as tricky as it can be with other fabrics). A steam iron and press cloth should be sufficient; if you have pressing arms, hams, or other tools, feel free to use them.

FIRST TEST YOUR MACHINE TENSION ON A SCRAP. Make sure that the thread tension on your machine isn't too tight, or it will cause puckering.

CARING FOR COTTON FABRICS

Cotton used in casual garments generally machine-washes well—provided it's been thoroughly preshrunk. However, in order to avoid any further shrinkage, it's best to line- or flat-dry cotton garments or tumble-dry with no or little heat, rather than tumble-drying on high. Super-fine and expensive cottons like you find in high-end shirting or dressier garments, however, should be dry-cleaned. Gently washing by hand might be acceptable, but test a swatch of the fabric to see if hand-washing alters it.

(TIP) If you make jeans (or other denim garments) from raw denim, borrow a trick from denim die-hards and don't wash them for at least a year. Instead, spot-clean stains or stick the jeans in the freezer overnight to deodorize them. This will preserve the color longer and allow the jeans to mold to your body and develop natural fade marks.

Above: Diane Keaton and Woody Allen's costumes in *Annie Hall* (1977) are classic examples of cotton at its best: tailored and put-together, yet casually rumpled.

Below is a guide to many of the most popular cotton fabrics, and some of the more unexpected ones. For the purposes of this chapter, the cotton fabrics described here have been arranged loosely by weight: first top weights, then medium weights, then bottom weights. However, keep in mind that some fabrics come in a variety of weights (in that case, a fabric is listed in the group where it's most commonly found) and that fabrics can be used outside of their typical range of styles for their weight, provided the garment will still be functional. (You could make a denim top, for instance, or an organdy anorak.)

TOP-WEIGHT COTTONS

These fabrics are light in weight, sometimes even very sheer, and are lovely for shirts, blouses, lingerie, sleepwear, and fuller dress styles. Depending on the garment you plan to make, you may need to plan on a lining; self-lining is often a good option with solid, lightweight cotton.

PLAIN WEAVE

More of a technical term than a specific fabric type, this catchall term means what it says: a plain-woven fabric in which the warp and weft yarns make a perfect one-by-one criss-cross pattern. Of course, plain weaves don't have to be plain, in the negative sense of the word. Plain-woven fabrics, because of their uniformity, make the best base for embroidery, and many types of luxurious fabrics in all fiber categories (taffeta, chiffon, voile) are plain-woven. Types of plain-weave cotton you might encounter include: **lawn,** a crisp and sometimes sheer shirting fabric; **batiste;** and **poplin** (see below).

BATISTE

One of the softest and drapiest of the shirting cottons, elegant batiste is cool to the touch. It makes lovely simple tops and lightweight shirts, and can also be used for summery lingerie. Because of its softness, many Mood customers use it as a lining for warm-weather tailored clothing. It's also sometimes referred to as **cambric;** both words are of French origin. Although it's not technically sheer, batiste can be translucent; try doubling up if you're making a dress or skirt.

VOILE

Voile is French for "veil," and that aptly sums up the look and feel of this lightweight cotton woven, which is similar to batiste but more translucent. Smooth, soft, and semi-sheer to sheer, voile makes for beautiful blouses, nighties, or overlayers, but it's not substantial enough to keep one's derriere covered.

Opposite:
1. Broadcloth
2. Poplin
3. Batiste
4. Cotton broadcloth
5. Poplin
6. Broadcloth
7. Poplin
8. Voile

BETTY SOLOMON

Eric's Right Hand, Social Media Manager, Buyer's Assistant, Mood NYC

Hometown:
Oxen Hill, Maryland (small suburb of Washington, D.C.)

Favorite fabric:
Cotton. "Cotton is just so versatile when you think about it, from jersey knit to sateen, and then poplins and voile."

Betty wears many hats at Mood. She's a fixture at the cash register. She's a buyer's assistant. She manages the social media accounts. And she does whatever else Eric needs. After moving to New York to pursue a career in radio, she slowly got back into styling and sewing some of her earlier passions, which led her to realize that she wanted to be involved with Mood in any way she could.

For Betty, the best part of the job is seeing what customers—from teenaged sewers to serious designers to stylists—do with the fabric they buy. On Pinterest, she started a board called "Made with Mood Fabrics." "I also like to follow up with people in person," Betty says. "They'll come back after a week or a month and say 'Remember this fabric?' and I'm like, 'Oh my, that's such a cute trench coat.'"

POPLIN AND BROADCLOTH
(SEE PHOTO PAGE 69)

These two classic shirting fabrics are quite similar; you can use them interchangeably in most cases.

Poplin is a smooth, tightly woven shirting fabric with a crisp, elegant feel and subtle sheen. It's generally woven with weft yarns thicker than warp yarns, a process that produces a very fine cross-grain rib texture. Its polished appearance and smooth hand make it ideal for fine dress shirts and more structured tops. Some fine poplins are marked with thread count, just like fine wool suitings. Poplin is also woven in heavier weights that are ideal for warm-weather sportswear pieces—it's a favorite in hot climates for men's suits.

Broadcloth is another tightly woven cotton, quite like poplin. Historically, the term broadcloth was used in England for a densely woven wool fabric treated to give it an almost felted hand. However, in the United States, broadcloth is the name used for a light-weight, smooth, cotton shirting fabric. Like poplin, broadcloth is an excellent choice for dressy shirts.

> "A high thread count doesn't always mean a poplin is better or stronger. Use your eyes and hands to get a feel for the fabric."
> —GEORGE COLEMAN, MOOD COTTONS EXPERT

OXFORD

One of those fabrics whose name has become interchangeable with a specific style of garment, **oxford** is a sturdy shirting material with a textured basketweave created through the combination of fine warp yarns and thicker weft yarns, sometimes in two different colors, producing a chambray-like effect. You may also find it in menswear-type patterns like stripes and tattersall checks. It's super-popular for casual shirts; think of the classic Brooks Brothers button-down, and you've got the idea. Oxford comes in a variety of weights, some of which work equally well for shirtdresses or casual skirts and shorts.

DOBBY AND PIQUÉ

The word **dobby** refers to a type of loom or loom attachment, and also any weave that contains small geometric shapes. Note that the patterns in a dobby weave are nowhere near as complex as those in a jacquard weave (see page 143); they're tiny and textural rather than bold and three-dimensional. Dobby cottons can be used for just about anything, from dresses to bedding, and offer more depth and texture than a plain weave.

Piqué is a type of dobby weave. Although there are many types of piqué weaves—often with waffle or honeycomb textures—a common one is called bird's-eye piqué; it's characterized by a tiny, raised diamond-shaped pattern. Piqué doesn't always have to be a daytime fabric: woven piqué with sheen makes for elegant shirting and ties, and in fact white piqué is a traditional choice for waistcoats, bow ties, and shirt fronts in "white tie" menswear. In heavier weights, piqué has a substantial and structural quality ideal for shift dresses and structured skirts.

Below:
1. Piqué
2. Oxford cloth
3. Dobby
4. Oxford cloth
5. Piqué
6. Chambray

QUILTING COTTON

As its name suggests, quilting cotton is generally intended for quilting. However, many sewers like to use this lightweight fabric for summer blouses and dresses because it comes in a variety of fun prints, colors, and patterns. (It's also generally quite affordable.) Quilting cotton tends to crease easily and be stiffer than many other apparel-quality cottons, but that can be part of its charm; use it for more structured styles, like sundresses or crisp tops. Note that quilting cottons come in a wide range of qualities. Some have a higher thread count and longer-staple cotton fiber, which makes for a smoother, silkier hand.

(TIP) Be sure to preshrink thoroughly. Quilting cotton hasn't necessarily been processed for use in apparel.

GAUZE AND CHEESECLOTH

Gauze has a much looser weave than voile and a unique crisscrossing weave structure that keeps it relatively stable. It also comes in wool, silk, and synthetic strains, though cotton is the most common. Although it's generally thought of as a humble fabric (and tends to be inexpensive), because of its transparency and ethereal look, it gathers and drapes beautifully. Designers with a penchant for drama, like Alexander McQueen and Rodarte, have used gathered, shredded, and raw-edged layers of gauze to romantic effect. Gauze sometimes comes with a crinkled finish; it can also be used for sheer shirting, or as an overlayer in a dress, skirt, or top, or bathing suit cover-up; stick with styles that have a good amount of ease, as gauze is too sheer and light for fitted, structured garments. (You can also generate more opacity in a garment by doubling up layers.)

Cheesecloth is a gauze-like cotton utility fabric generally used for things other than fashion—namely, cheesemaking—and often sold in different thread densities for specific industrial applications. Some gauzes in a fabric store might be labeled as cheesecloth.

(TIPS)

• The open weave of gauzy fabrics means you'll need to handle them a little differ-

Below: Quilting cotton
1–2. Gingham
3. Cotton print
4–5. Cotton floral

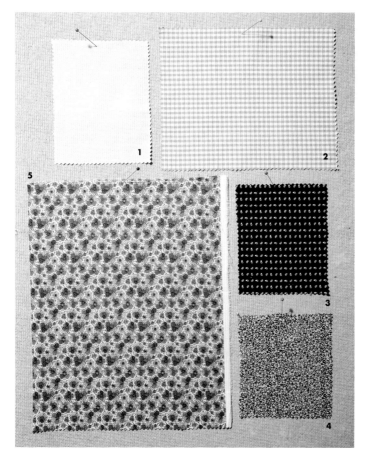

Above: Sheers
(left to right):

Dotted swiss
Cotton gauze
Cotton gauze
Cotton cheesecloth
Cotton organdy

ORGANDY

The old-fashioned fabric of starched petticoats and Victorian sundresses, organdy is the cotton counterpart to organza; it's made by subjecting plain weave cotton lawn to an acid bath. Crisp and sheer just like its silk counterpart, organdy is often used as the base for embroidery and lace. Use it as an outermost layer in dreamy summer dresses or sheer shell tops; or as sew-in interfacing; or to create dramatic ruffles, flounces, and volume, on its own or beneath another fabric.

(TIPS)

• Use a smaller needle, such as 60/8 or 70/10, for this delicate fabric.

• Organdy can be slippery in the sewing machine. Hand-basting the seam allowances keeps separate pieces in line.

DOTTED SWISS

This top-weight textile, named after the country where its design originated, is a lightweight, sometimes sheer cotton shirting (usually batiste or voile) with a napped dot design. It has a sweet, innocent feel that's perfect for feminine blouses and ruffle trims—but some designers subvert this expectation by whipping it up into tomboyish or edgy silhouettes. Beware of inexpensive varieties that are simply lightweight cotton with flock-printed dots. They won't wear as well (or look as elegant) as actual dotted swiss.

(TIP) The dots of dotted swiss have a nap with a direction, so be sure that the nap is facing the same way when you cut pattern pieces.

ently from tighter, smoother textiles. Wash gauze and let it dry before cutting and sewing. Use a steamer and your hands to coax it back to its original state if it has crinkles.

• Gauze and cheesecloth tend to grow during sewing. Use paper or seam-stabilizer tape (see Silks chapter, page 124) to stabilize seam areas.

• Gauzes also fray like crazy, so finish seams cleanly with bias tape or as French seams.

• Crinkled gauze can be tricky to cut. Use pins (in the seam allowance areas) instead of weights, as weights might flatten out the fabric temporarily.

These intermediate-weight textiles are versatile: Use them for heavier tops, outerwear, skirts, and trousers, depending on the particular fabric. If you think your fabric is a bit too light for a bottom garment or a hardwearing accessory like a tote bag, consider adding heft with a lightweight cotton underlining (see page 44).

> "I found a two-dollar flannel shirt on St. Mark's Place and I sent it off to Italy and had it made into $300-a-yard plaid silk."
>
> —MARC JACOBS, ON HIS INFAMOUS 1992 "GRUNGE" COLLECTION

SATEEN

Sateen is the cotton equivalent of satin, and its name applies to cottons and other non-silk satin-weave fabrics only. The shiny side works for shirting, or in heavier weights, as a more structured alternative to silk satin in jackets, dresses, or even bottoms (sateens blended with a touch of stretch fiber are popular for this purpose). Flipping the sheen to the inside creates a smooth feeling against the skin; for this reason, sateen also makes a great lining. Some sateens have also been **mercerized,** though not every type of mercerized cotton is sateen. That process, invented by John Mercer in 1844, involves a chemical bath that gives cotton and other fibers a softer, smoother feel and greater resilience.

Opposite: Medium-weight cottons (top to bottom):

Cotton flannel
Moleskin
Moleskin
Cotton flannel
Sateen
Sateen
Sateen

FLANNEL

Fuzzy, cozy flannel is a favorite for pajamas, bedding, robes, and button-down shirts. Flannel is a medium- to heavyweight plain weave marked by a brushed, napped surface, and also comes in a wool version. The cotton variety tends to pill, so is often best saved for loungewear and casual garments. It's also appropriate for use as an interlining in outerwear, or as an underlining for structured bodices. Cotton flannel may be brushed on one or both sides.

(TIP) It may be subtle, but flannel's nap has a direction. Be sure to cut all pieces with the nap facing the same way.

MOLESKIN

Moleskin is a sturdy, structured cotton fabric that mimics the skin of a mole, which means it's lightly fuzzy and cozy. The fabric is woven and then sheared to create a subtle, close-cut, nap with a matte finish. A refreshingly understated alternative to corduroy or suede, it makes a comfortable, chic fabric for fall jackets, jeans, pants, bags, or anything for which you might use corduroy or velveteen. While soft, it's also dense and durable, which is why it's also used in medical and podiatric applications to line shoes and prevent blisters.

(TIP) As subtle as the nap may appear, don't cut corners when cutting—be sure to arrange pattern pieces so the nap faces the same way.

mood INC

DESIGNER FABRIC
225 West 37th Street   3rd Floor
New York, NY 10018
(212)730-5003 • Fax: 221-1932

PLAIDS AND GINGHAM

Plaid's crisscrossing patterns are traditionally yarn-dyed, meaning that the yarn is dyed before being woven into fabric, although some plaid patterns are now printed on the surface of fabric. The effect can be preppy or punk, depending on the design. Lightweight cotton with a plaid pattern is often referred to as **madras**—a summery and usually colorful type of check, named for its origin in colonial India where it was originally dyed with unstable vegetable dyes. These days, madras plaid evokes the charm of golf links, country clubs, and mint juleps. Some madras plaids are reconfigured into clever patchwork, by stitching squares of different plaid colors together—an especially iconic look for summer shorts.

Gingham didn't originate as a strictly checked fabric, but by now it's synonymous with a two-color picnic-tablecloth pattern. A medium-weight plain weave with a crisp hand, gingham achieved pop-culture immortality via Judy Garland's Dorothy in *The Wizard of Oz*. Gingham may be thought of as sweet and innocent (or countrified), but a more chic example is the mid-century French screen siren Brigitte Bardot, who got married in 1959 in a pink gingham dress and rocked many variations of the fabric on- and off-screen: full skirts, tiny tops and shorts, hourglass-shaped dresses. So timeless was the gingham-based look she sported on the boardwalks of Saint-Tropez that Karl Lagerfeld designed an entire resort collection around it in 2010.

(TIP) Take extra care with your cutting layout. Plaid patterns should be matched at adjoining seams for a continuous, professional appearance.

Opposite: Various stripes, plaids, and black-and-white gingham

Right: Gingham has a sweet reputation, but even old-fashioned fabrics can be twisted into something edgy, as seen in Comme des Garçons's infamous "bump" collection from season spring/ summer 1997.

SEERSUCKER

Stripes plus puckers equal seersucker, but that's not the origin of the name: It actually comes from the Hindi term "kheer aur shakkar," meaning "rice pudding and sugar," which aptly describes the fabric's texture. A summer fabric, cotton seersucker was popularized by Brits in colonial India and still retains a gentlemanly, preppy air. It's known for being cool to wear and wrinkle-resistant, even in the most sweltering climate. While it's perennially popular for summer suits and bow ties, striped seersucker can also be used for dresses, jackets, and shorts—even, sometimes, with a hint of irony. It also comes in varieties other than one-by-one colored stripes, like gingham seersucker, solid seersucker made of shiny and dull stripes, or even printed seersucker.

CHAMBRAY
(SEE PHOTO PAGE 71)

A kindred spirit of denim, chambray is technically a closer relative to cambric, and both originated in the French city of Cambrai. Chambray is a soft, medium-weight plain-weave fabric marked by a white weft and a colored (usually pale blue) warp. Its subtle shading makes it an iconic choice for casual shirts and shirtdresses with top-stitched seams and pockets, and it pairs beautifully with jeans.

Opposite: Seersucker fabrics.

MUSLIN
(SEE PHOTO PAGE 64)

If you've taken a fashion design class, you've learned about "making a muslin"— that is, a prototype created to fit the pattern before cutting the final garment. The fabric most often used for this process goes by the same name. A stiff, plain-woven, unprocessed cotton, **muslin**—in the modern and American sense of the word—is a staple of home sewing rooms and couture ateliers alike. This is because it's both cheap and easy to sew. ("Muslin" has also become shorthand for any fabric used to make a prototype, regardless of whether it's muslin.) Aside from testing purposes, muslin is also used for tote bags and the protective drawstring bags that come with shoes and leather handbags. Because it's unprocessed, it hasn't been preshrunk, which makes it a poor candidate for clothes intended for wear, or for sew-in interfacing. If you do make something other than a prototype or basic bag with it, wash and machine-dry the fabric twice before cutting.

In British English, muslin is called **calico.** Historically, the term "muslin" has also referred to cotton gauze, which in ancient Bengal was woven in quite luxurious forms. However, in most cases, if you see something called muslin, it's being sold for prototyping purposes.

(TIP) Muslin is subject to extreme shrinkage. Avoid steaming during the design and fitting process. And for this reason, try not to let it crease too much—keep your muslin prototype on a hanger, out of harm's way.

GEORGE COLEMAN

Sales Associate,
Cottons, Mood NYC

Hometown:
Oakland, California

Favorite fabric:
Denim. "It can be
casual or it can
be a tuxedo. It can
be cheap, or as
expensive as a
fine silk jacquard.
There's no limit."

"As a kid, art was my big thing," says George. But he set his sights on fashion as a teenager after he got his hands on his older sister's fashion magazines. "I realized, hey, this is creative," he says. Obsessed with Armani (it was the '80s, after all), George crossed the country to attend the Fashion Institute of Technology in New York. After graduation, he spent two decades designing blouses, denim, and casual wear for a series of Seventh Avenue stalwarts: to name a few, Brooks Brothers, Talbots, and Bill Blass ("he worked me like a damn horse," George says).

In 2006, feeling "a bit tired" from the designer grind, he joined Mood, which enabled him to build a design consulting business on the side, thanks to his proximity to the world's best selection of fabric and a steady stream of designer customers. Many of the young designers who come in to buy fabric from George also need help with executing their visions technically; they need introductions to the right sample rooms and production houses to help grow their businesses. Some home sewers dream of starting a side project; others just need a custom-fitted suit. As a Garment District veteran who knows every patternmaker and factory owner in town, George is always happy to go the extra mile for his Mood customers. "I can't tell you how many young designers I have met through Mood will call me and say, 'George, come to my first show!'" he says. "The best thing about my job is feeling like a real part of the designer community."

According to George, the constraints of commerce are actually good for creativity. "Once you understand that you're not just designing for yourself," he says, "it can be satisfying to problem-solve and then add your own personal elements to keep it fresh. I had to balance the technical side and the creative side in the sportswear business, and that skill has stayed with me to this day." To wit, he's been busy designing everything from gloves to dog T-shirts. "Trying to design a T-shirt for a dog gives you a lot to think about!" he laughs. "Working in new formats makes you stretch your wings."

BOTTOM-WEIGHT COTTONS

As the name suggests, these textiles are ideal for skirts and trousers. However, you'll find them appropriate for jackets and coats as well. Because heavier cotton fabrics aren't known for their drape, look for garment designs with structure and shape.

TWILL WEAVES

Technically a type of weave, **twill** refers to a class of fabrics distinguished by diagonal ribs (which appear like diagonal lines on the face of the fabric). Their weave structure makes them durable and more tear- and stain-resistant than flat-surfaced plain-weave fabrics, which is why they are associated with work wear and casual, no-nonsense pants and shirts. **Chino,** often simply referred to as "twill," is one common form of this type of fabric, used early on for hard-wearing British and American military uniforms, and now often used for casual pants (hence their name) and jackets. **Gabardine** is a water-resistant outerwear twill invented by Thomas Burberry in 1879 and used for trench coats and jackets. **Drill** is even tougher, and its military name hints at its no-nonsense nature. It comes in a variety of weights, designed for anything from army shirts to boat sails.

Five different denims
followed by brown
drill, beige drill, and
beige chino.

DENIM

So iconic is the fabric of blue jeans that it deserves its own book (and many have, in fact, been written). Denim is a coarse fabric in the twill family, often distinguished by an indigo hue, but it's so much more than that: It's the official fabric of cool. Its name is thought to be a derivation of *serge de Nîmes*, after the textile center of Nîmes, France, though some scholars believe the fabric originated in England. Traditional denim is woven with dark (usually blue) warp yarns and white weft yarns; the blue yarns are visible on the fabric's right side, while the white yarns show on the wrong side. (A similar, solid-colored fabric called "jean" also emerged from Italy and England around the same time.) In the 19th century, the San Francisco entrepreneur Levi Strauss created riveted denim pants for miners to wear, and the rest is fashion history. Farmers, cowboys, rebels, movie stars, hippies, and rock stars have proudly worn blue jeans, and today just about everyone has a pair (or a drawer full). Of course, denim also makes for great jackets, skirts, and bags and small accessories, and it needn't be styled like classic jeans (that is, with orange thread and rivets). Denim has an air of authenticity and rugged individualism, thanks to its natural fade, unique among textiles. This is created by indigo denim's dark and light yarns. Washing and wear reveal more and more of the white yarns over time.

There are as many varieties of denim as there are styles of jeans. Denim can be heavyweight or lightweight, all cotton or a blend of cotton plus synthetics like spandex, stretch four ways or be stiff as sandpaper. It also comes in solid colors, which won't fade in the same way but can make for interesting alternatives to blue jeans.

(TIP) With its lovely, variegated pale-blue hue, the "wrong" side of indigo denim can be an interesting and unexpected choice for the outside of a garment—or try using both sides to color-block a jacket or jeans.

> **"[Blue jeans] are the most beautiful things since the gondola."**
>
> —DIANA VREELAND, *VOGUE* EDITOR-IN-CHIEF

MAKING REAL JEANS

Sewing denim isn't difficult, but it's a thick and dense fabric that requires some special techniques and supplies. To make a really authentic pair of jeans, follow these guidelines.

- Needless to say, use a denim needle! Heavy-duty thread is also recommended. Many jeans feature a specific orange or gold shade of heavyweight thread in topstitched areas.

- Denim frays— that's why cutoffs are great, but it's not such a good quality when it comes to your seams. Sturdy flat-fell seams are the most durable for jeans; single seams can pop open more easily. If that's not an option, use a serger or bias tape to enclose raw edges, and run a second line of stitching in high-stress areas like the hips and crotch.

- Don't make jeans' pocket bags out of denim; they'll add bulk where you don't want it. Use plain-weave cotton or flannel instead.

- Rivets need not be left to the pros. Use a hammer and nail to pound a hole in the jeans first; you may need to add a couple of layers of denim to the rivet as spacers. Make sure the rivet is going in straight before you hammer it all the way into its cap.

> "Most denim is preshrunk to a degree, but you can still expect up to 10% shrinkage. Do a wash and dry test on a 10"x 10" (25 cm x 25 cm) piece of fabric first. And don't try to preshrink a huge 10-yard piece of fabric all at once, or you'll destroy your washing machine."

—GEORGE COLEMAN, MOOD COTTONS EXPERT

Above: Classic denim silhouettes like jeans and a jean jacket can be a starting point for creating new shapes, as this look from Jean Paul Gaultier's spring/summer 2013 collection demonstrates.

TUTORIAL: HAND-WEATHERING YOUR JEANS

Old-school jeans started as raw indigo denim and got their subtle fades and rips from years of wear and tear on the ranch or motorcycle. But today, most jeans are pre-distressed in the factory using high-tech tools like sandblaster guns. Denim fabric can sometimes come in faded shades of blue and gray, but whiskers, holes, softened corners, and all the other markers of well-loved jeans can only be added once the garment is sewn. Those seeking a broken-in look right off the bat need not shy away from sewing their own jeans, though: It's easy to fake it till your blues make it.

- Study the fade pattern of a pair of worn-in jeans you already love. If desired, use a disappearing ink fabric marker to mark whisker placement.

- Place a pillow or towel inside the jeans and use sandpaper to sand down general areas for fading, as well as small areas like pocket corners.

- To create a whisker, first turn the jeans inside out. Place a pencil crosswise inside the jeans around the crotch area, using another pair of jeans as a guide for placement, then tape it at both ends to secure. Turn the jeans right side out, and sand gently so that the sandpaper touches the jeans along the ridge of the pencil. Repeat as needed.

- To fade the overall color of indigo jeans, make a solution of 1 part chlorine bleach to 3 parts water. Dampen the jeans in water first, then submerge them in the bleach solution. Leave them to soak, checking every 15 minutes until the desired color is attained. Then wash them with detergent.

DENIM ON THE EDGE

SELVAGE DENIM is a type of premium denim favored by jean fetishists and high-end fashion labels. Often originating in Japan, it's distinguished by a selvage edge that usually sports a red line. It's woven on old looms, and in widths that are quite a bit narrower than other denims—often as narrow as 32" (81 cm) wide—so you'll need to purchase a longer length. Use it for straight-leg patterns (this is more common for men's styles, but not unheard-of for women's jeans; you may want to do some light patternmaking if you want this style to fit the female form). Line up the side seams of the main pattern pieces along the selvage edge and make this your seam allowance. Because the edge is self-finished, your jeans will be, too; press the seam allowances open and cuff the jeans to show off this detail.

CORDUROY

Not many fabrics have entire social organizations devoted to celebrating their merits, but corduroy is one of those fabrics that inspires nostalgia and full-out love. The Corduroy Appreciation Club, founded in 2006, sponsored large gatherings of corduroy-clad New Yorkers on dates with "11" in them before unraveling, so to speak, shortly after its crowning event on 11/11/11.

Associated with scholars, prepsters, and '70s daywear, corduroy features napped rows, called wales, that range from very wide to very fine. (The wale count refers to the number of wales per inch; a smaller number means a wider wale.) Though it's most commonly used for suits and pants, corduroy comes in a variety of weights that can work for structured dresses, jackets, and even bags and small accessories. It also makes for a great accent or contrast fabric on pockets, yokes, and plackets.

(TIPS)

- Corduroy has a nap, so be sure when cutting that all pieces face the same direction.
- Press on the wrong side to avoid flattening the wales.
- Topstitch from the right side only; the feed dogs might leave permanent marks on the wales if you stitch corduroy with the right side down.

VELVETEEN AND COTTON VELVET

Though velvet is usually made of silk or synthetics, some types are made with cotton, in which case they will be less shiny than the standard variety. **Velveteen** is a specific type of short-pile cotton velvet that has a stiffer, crisper hand and substantial body. It makes for an ideal bottom- or jacket-weight fabric for tailored day or evening looks.

(TIP) Like silk velvets, cotton velvets will make a mess when you cut them. They also have a nap, so be sure when cutting that all pieces face the same direction.

Below: Cotton corduroys in various wale widths
Opposite: Cotton velvet swatches and velveteen (far right)

COTTON'S COUSINS: LINEN AND HEMP FABRICS

Linen, the fiber of the flax plant, has been in use since prehistoric times. In ancient Egypt, it was considered a symbol of light, purity, and wealth, and used for both currency and wrapping cloths for mummification. Still priced as something of a luxury today, due to its long fiber length and labor-intensive spinning process, linen is renowned for its coolness in hot weather, and the way it softens beautifully over time while remaining exceptionally durable. Linen is a **bast fiber**, which means it comes from the long threads in the stem of the plant; this gives it its distinctive irregular texture. Because it lets cool air circulate against the skin—and because it wrinkles like mad, which is part of its charm—it's best used for fluid, not fitted, silhouettes. The effect creates an elegantly rumpled summer look for suiting, jackets, tops, skirts, and dresses. Seek out **Belgian linen**; that country's mills are renowned for the beautiful linen fabrics they produce.

The term "linens" can also refer to anything from bedding to towels. The word shares the same root as many others: *lingerie* (which was once made from linen), *line* (linen cords or threads were used to delineate straight paths), and *lining* (because suiting was once commonly lined with, you guessed it, linen). Cottons and other fibers made with a textured **linen weave**, or blended with linen, are often grouped with linen and used for similar styles.

(TIPS)

- Beware of wrinkles, which can throw off pattern pieces during cutting. Press linen fabric with a hot steam iron before cutting, and handle very carefully during sewing to avoid creating new creases.
- Linen can fray, and therefore behaves best with clean-finished or serged hems.

HEMP

Banish any associations with psychoactive substances: hemp, the fiber of the cannabis plant, is one of the most durable and environmentally beneficial textiles around. It's considered a sustainable fabric due to the fact that it doesn't need much fertilizer or pesticides to grow and improves soil quality. Hemp, as a bast fiber, tends to resemble linen in its slightly nubby texture. It most often comes in canvas or herringbone weaves, and is sometimes blended with cotton or silk to create a softer product. It's also used to make denim and even slub jersey for T-shirts. Mood doesn't carry a huge variety, but sometimes a good-quality hemp from a designer's showroom will find its way to the shelves. At other fabric stores or online retailers, you might also find hemp sold undyed as greige goods, which means it's not processed or shrunk; be sure to ask a salesperson if you aren't sure.

Just how strong is hemp? In addition to making great tote bags and casual outerwear and pants, it's used for heavy-duty ropes, paper, industrial fabrics, and even building materials and plastics.

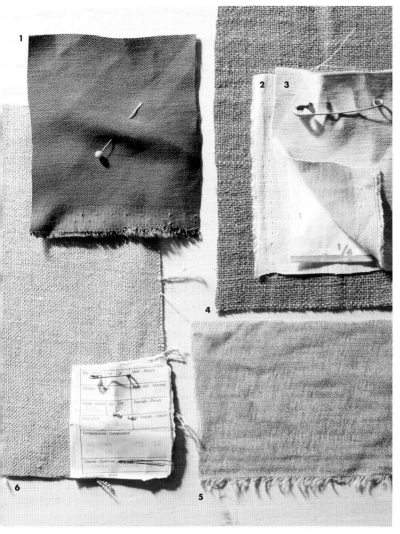

Above:
1–4. 100% linen
5. Open-weave hemp
6. Belgian linen

"I don't think that 'eco' should be a word that immediately conjures up images of oatmeal-colored garments or garments that are oversized or lacking in any sort of luxury or beauty or detailing or desirability. I don't think that things have to look ugly because they're organic; why can't they be beautiful as well?"

—STELLA MCCARTNEY, DESIGNER

//

JOE VARON

Sales Associate, Cotton Department, Mood NYC

Hometown:
Teaneck, New Jersey

Favorite fabric:
"My favorite fabric is the fabric that sells."

//

Joe is straightforward about his job—"I sell fabrics." And he's been doing this for more than 25 years. He started "fairly early" as a way to make a living. And he's now become a fixture at Mood, knowledgeable about all fabric types. After his previous employer went out of business, he moved to Mood and has been here since 2001. While Joe's focus is now cotton, he's worked in the wool and silk departments too.

Joe enjoys the fast pace of the store, talking to his customers, helping them find what they need, and cutting it. "We know the fabrics that are here. We pull out the fabric, we sell it. In and out. It's cut and dry."

Wools

FOR AS LONG AS HUMANS and animals have lived side by side, people have used animal fiber to create textiles. Wool, as a category, refers to the family of protein-based fabrics made from animal hairs spun into yarn and woven into fabric. Though fabrics from sheep and lamb fleece are the most common (and generally the most affordable), the wool category can also cover **cashmere** and **mohair** (also called angora) from goats; **angora** rabbit hair (often blended with lambswool or other fibers); **alpaca** (from llamas); **camel hair**; and other exotic types like **vicuña** wool and **qiviut**, the wool of musk oxen, as well as blends thereof.

Wool is synonymous with warmth in winter, but it encompasses so much more than heavy coats and blankets. Because it wicks moisture away from the skin and because its crimped texture traps air, wool isn't merely cozy and warm in cold weather; it's also cooling in hot weather (and desert nomadic tribes, such as Bedouins, use it for that very purpose). It is, of course, the fabric of choice for fall and winter coats and jackets, but woven wool is also ideal for fine suiting and tailored pants, dresses, and skirts. In its finer, softer, lighter-weight varieties, wool can also make for beautiful, delicate blouses and shawls. The advent of summer-weight wools (like **tropical wool**, a type of summer suiting) and easy-care washable wools means that the fabric can be used for just about anything—at just about any time of year.

Sheep have been domesticated since around 10,000 B.C. in Europe and the Middle East. The earliest people spun crude yarns with their fingers to form unevenly textured cloths. With the advent of shears and the spinning wheel, which enabled the production of yarns for weaving, wool cloth spread in popularity. Wool was commonly used for clothing throughout ancient Rome and medieval Europe; later, in the 19th and 20th centuries, it was the center of the economy in colonial Australia. Its cultivation has been so important to the British economy and culture that since the 14th century, the Lord Speaker of the House of Lords has sat on the Woolsack, a seat stuffed with wool meant to represent the supremacy of the wool trade. Nowadays, most of the world's wool comes from Australia and New Zealand. (In New Zealand, sheep even outnumber people.)

SEWING WOOL FABRICS

Wool wovens are generally easy to cut and sew and resist wrinkling, but as with every type of fabric, there are ways to make the most of wool's distinctive qualities.

MIND YOUR SHRINKAGE. Wool, especially wool crepe, shrinks a great deal if you wash it in water. Moisture and agitation cause the individual fibers' scales to interlock and mat, so the fabric takes on a denser, **felted** quality. The safest way to preshrink sheets of wool fabric before cutting is to have a dry cleaner steam-press them. You can do this yourself at home, but it is time-consuming (see sidebar opposite). With wool fabric that's already felted or labeled washable, you might instead prewash the uncut yardage in cold water

> ## "If I could only use one fiber, it would be wool. You can't beat that versatility, from coziness to absolute luxury."
>
> —MICHAEL KORS

Previous pages: Left to right: Matte wool jersey; black-and-cream wool draped by Errick Perryman.

with a detergent meant to be used with wool before cutting. Discuss with your fabric salesperson if you're not sure whether a fabric will look different after prewashing, and if in doubt, steam-press instead.

KEEP IT SIMPLE—WITH SOME EXCEPTIONS. The finest wools aside (like worsted ultrafine suiting, challis, and voile), much wool is on the thicker side and doesn't really lend itself to intricate draping and gathering. Creating volume in thicker fabrics results in unflattering bulk on the body and is difficult to sew, too.

CHOOSE THE RIGHT NEEDLE FOR YOUR PROJECT. Many light-to-medium-weight wools will do just fine with a universal needle in size 80/12. Thicker coatings require a heavier needle, and fine voile and challis could benefit from something smaller or a Microtex/sharp needle.

CARING FOR WOOL FABRICS

Even if you've preshrunk your woolen textile, there's still potential for it to shrink and felt if washed. For this reason, and also because wool fabrics are often made into structured garments with many supporting layers of different textiles, you'll find it worthwhile to take extra care in cleaning and storing clothes made of wool.

DRY-CLEAN ONLY—USUALLY. Mood's official stance on caring for wool is that, unless a wool fabric is specifically labeled as washable wool, the safest bet is to leave the cleaning of the finished garment to the pros. That said, there are detergents specially designed for the care of wool. If—and only if—you've preshrunk the fabric used for a garment and the garment is flexible and lightweight, as in some worsted wools, you might be safe hand-washing it in cold water with Woolite, baby shampoo, or the no-rinse products Soak or Eucalan. Don't try this with large, heavy garments (they'll weigh a ton when wet!), tailored suiting, or anything that needs to retain a perfect shape—or any form of wool crepe, which shrinks substantially. When in doubt, send it out.

WATCH OUT FOR MOTHS. The larvae of moths and carpet beetles love to chew holes in your beautiful wool clothes—and the same issue applies to uncut fabric. Use cedar inserts in drawers and closets, and store wool garments and fabric sheets in airtight tubs. Periodically unfold and inspect your stored fabrics, too; pests don't like being bothered. If you live in a climate where moths are a problem, don't store your wool fabric for too long before making use of it, or you might be in for a holey surprise. Should you discover that something has been nibbling at your fabric, but you can still salvage enough for a garment, first get rid of any potential eggs by either tumbling the yardage in a hot dryer or placing it in the freezer for a couple of days. You can also salvage moth-eaten fabric by washing and felting it, which sometimes—if the holes are small enough—closes them up. This will, however, result in a thicker, denser material than what you started with. Of course, you'll need to check your storage area to get rid of any remaining insects (or larvae).

STEAM-SHRINKING WOOL FABRICS

A good at-home method to preshrink wool fabric is to use a combination of moisture and heat. Get the yardage damp (lay it all out and spray with water; wash a sheet, lay it out damp, lay the wool fabric on it, roll it up and wrap it in plastic for several hours or overnight), then unroll it and press it with a hot, dry iron, till it's dry. Press it section by section, letting each bit cool and dry before moving to the next section.

Wools come in a variety of weights, weave structures, and textures. For ease of reference, this chapter examines wool fabrics (and their properties and uses) in alphabetical order. However, wool fabrics that are often interchangeable or associated with one another (such as suiting and worsted wool, which overlap as categories) are grouped together. At Mood, as in most fabric stores, different types of wools are subdivided by weight into groups for SUITING, SHIRTING, and COATING.

Cashmere and exotics (such as camel hair and alpaca) are addressed separately at the end of the chapter.

LEARNING FROM COCO CHANEL

Chanel had a special lining technique that retained the almost sweater-like drape of her signature cardigan jackets: She quilted silk charmeuse to the bouclé, rather than using a separate lining. She did this with bouclé skirts, too. This way, the lining supported the loose weave of the bouclé, which otherwise might have a tendency to droop, sag, or develop snags and pulls.

DESIGN TIPS

Bouclé loves to fray—but sometimes this can be its own design element. Chanel, for instance, features exposed seam allowances and raw hems on many of its bouclé styles. Just be sure to run a line of stitching along any hem to prevent the entire garment from unraveling!

BOUCLÉ

The French word for "curly," bouclé is a novelty fabric made with looped, curly yarns, creating a rich, multi-dimensional texture. Many bouclés are blends that include synthetic and metallic fibers in addition to wool and silk. Bouclé was the signature fabric of Coco Chanel, and continues to be an inspired choice for classic little jackets, as well as skirts, pants, and outerwear. Choose richly textured bouclés with a deep pile—rather than flat, itchy varieties with all synthetic content—for the most high-end, fashion-forward look.

(TIP) Bouclé is meant to be lined, in most cases; it doesn't always feel great against the skin. Because of its texture, the seam allowances may fray like mad, but a lining will keep them out of sight and out of mind. If you leave a bouclé jacket unlined, use bias binding to cover raw seam edges.

Opposite: An assortment of bouclés

Above: Lightweight wools (left to right):
Challis
Voile
Gauze

CHALLIS, VOILE, AND GAUZE

When we think of wool, we often think of bulky winter garments, but wool can also be downright ethereal. These top-weight fabrics make beautiful, delicate blouses, sophisticated dresses, or can be used to make the world's easiest accessory: scarves. **Challis** is a lightweight, drapey, breathable, all-purpose plain weave that also comes in rayon and polyester versions (but the Mood staff favors pure, natural wool). It's a perennial favorite for tops and blouses, but it can sometimes come in bottom weights, too, which make for lovely skirts and pants. **Wool voile**, like cotton voile, has a smooth finish and translucent quality. **Wool gauze,** like cotton gauze, is an open weave. Try using it for decorative top layers to add an element of transparency, or gather and drape it for dramatic effect.

(TIPS)

• These fabrics are the most delicate of all wools. Avoid using them for anything structured and close-fitting, or the seams will get stressed out.

• Remember that many challises, voiles, and gauzes have an element of transparency. Try double-layering for opacity.

• Because of their sheerness and tendency to fray, lightweight wools work best with clean-finished seams. Try French seams or bias binding rather than pinking shears or a serger.

TUTORIAL:
WOOL SHAWL

Make an easy, elegant scarf from soft wool challis or voile. Simply cut out a perfect square in the size of your choosing, run a line of stitching around the edge (leaving at least ½" [12 mm] seam allowance). If desired, clean-finish the vertical (parallel to the selvage) edges with double-fold hems. Pull out the loose threads from the raw edges until you have even fringe. Trim any straggling threads, and you've got yourself a chic, all-purpose accessory. Try hand-painting with dye, tie-dyeing, or dip-dyeing the fabric for extra credit, but be aware that the fabric will shrink and felt somewhat when washed or dunked in hot dye.

Right: Checks and plaids
(clockwise from top left):

Houndstooth
Tartan
Glen plaid (a.k.a. Prince
   of Wales plaid)
Wool shirting

DESIGN TIP
Play with cutting plaids
on the bias for details
such as yokes, pockets,
or skirt flounces. The
contrast creates a bold,
graphic look and adds
depth to your design.

CHECKS AND PLAIDS

Plaid fabric has a rich history in Europe and especially in Scotland, where it's known as **tartan**. Different patterns woven by different weavers (usually in wool) became identifiers for residents of different regions and, starting in the 19th century, specific clans registered their own tartans. (It's still possible to do so today through the Scottish Register of Tartans.) Plaid wool shirting was popularized in the United States by Pendleton Woolen Mills in 1924; the company is a now a beloved part of American fashion heritage, and its signature shirt is as sought-after as ever today. Checks and plaids can be classic or subversive, preppy or punk, depending on the design.

(TIP) Take extra care with your cutting layout. Plaid patterns should be matched at adjoining seams for a continuous, professional appearance. To effectively match plaids, you are likely to need slightly more yardage—about ¼ to ½ yard (23 cm to 46 cm) extra per garment.

CREPE

The delicate texture and depth of crepe looks particularly rich rendered in wool, which is why this light- to medium-weight fabric is popular for just about everything, from blouses to heavy coats. Wool crepe can take a number of forms, but it is generally woven of yarn that has been twisted, resulting in a subtle, grainy or textured surface. When the yarns are made from smooth, shiny worsted wool, it has the drape and sheen of suiting, and makes for beautiful blazers, skirts, and trousers. Fuzzier woolen crepes can come in top weights, bottom weights, and coating. Crepe is incredibly versatile, but there's one thing to remember about it: It shrinks like crazy. Preshrinking, therefore, is crucial. Do not, we repeat, do not machine-wash it, unless you're after a felted look. (And do not machine-wash your finished garment.)

(TIP) Crepe tends to fray. Clean-finish seams, or in the case of tailored garments, use a lining to cover up the evidence.

DOUBLE-FACED WOOL

Wool is sometimes found in **double-faced** varieties. This textile is actually two fabrics in one, woven with a set of threads that join the fabrics, wrong sides together. This means that both sides are considered the face, and both can be incorporated into the design—ideal for reversible and unlined styles, interesting draping and folds, or cuffs to be rolled up. Double-faced wools have a luxurious look, and are a perennial favorite of runway designers. They're mostly found in the coating category, though some thinner or worsted wools—suitable for luxurious fall/winter trousers, skirts, jackets, and dresses—line the shelves at Mood. The two-sided feature can be an interesting design element for just about any garment, so play away!

(TIP) To finish the hems of a double-faced wool garment, pull the layers apart at the edge; you'll see that they are attached by threads throughout the body. You can then fold each hem allowance in, and slipstitch the edges together.

Opposite: Wool crepe
Below: Double-faced wool

FELTED AND BOILED WOOLS

When wool is washed, it takes on a **felted** quality. The kinky fibers scrunch up and interlock, filling the gaps between yarns with fuzz and shrinking the fabric. In the case of felted wool, this is deliberate, and the washing happens before it gets to the store. The combination of moisture, heat, friction, and pressure that's used is also called **fulling**. One advantage of felted wool is that the seams can be left unfinished; the dense structure of the felted fibers means the fabric won't fray. Many felted-wool garment designs take full advantage of this, leaving coats unlined and hems raw. Another benefit of felted wool is that it can be extremely warm, since the felting creates a barrier against wind while keeping a garment breathable.

One common felted wool is **melton**, a heavyweight coating with a napped outer surface that's popular for winter coats (think of navy-style peacoats). **Boiled wool,** common in traditional German jacket styles, is lighter in weight and traditionally made by boiling knitted fabric—though once felted, it behaves more like a woven. It tends to have a curly surface texture, and is often used unlined for a sweater-like coat option. Both are excellent outerwear options for structured looks, but probably wouldn't be useful for much else. **Wool felt** is a nonwoven fabric, but it can be treated like a woven in cutting and sewing. It has no warp or weft, only yarns mashed together, and it too can be left raw without risk of unraveling.

Thanks to their inherent stability, these fabrics don't usually need interfacing or lining. However, they're also thick and heavy, and seam allowances in a standard, right-sides-together seam can get bulky. Consider trying either a **lapped seam** (one layer overlapping another, both with right sides up, and topstitched) or, for the supplest allowances, an **abutted seam** (seam allowances removed, and garment sections aligned with cut edges touching; a flatlock or wide zigzag joins the pieces side by side).

(TIPS)

- Use a heavier needle for thicker felted wools, up to 100/16 (depending on the exact weight of your fabric). Don't attempt to work with felted wool on a dinky, cheap sewing machine. Only quality machines are able to handle its heft.
- Try using Teflon presser feet for greater ease of sewing.
- Buttonholes can be tricky on thick felted fabrics. Make a few test buttonholes on a scrap; if you don't like the results, you can try adding cording loops, toggles, ties, a bold zipper, or some other creative closure.

Opposite:
1. Melton
2. Wool felt
3–4. Boiled wool

FLANNEL

More polished and high-end in feel than its cotton cousin, wool flannel also features a brushed nap on a plain or twill weave. While cotton tends to look pilly and rumpled after repeated washing, wool flannel has a more tailored, drapey elegance that lends itself to trousers, blazers, and even dresses. Charcoal-gray flannel, with or without a pinstripe, is a classic for men's cold-weather suits. In a bold plaid, it's great for rugged shirts and Pendleton-style shirt-jackets.

(TIP) Even if you can't see it, flannel's nap has a direction. Cut all pattern pieces in the same direction to avoid variations in shade on the finished garment.

MERINO WOOL

Sometimes you'll see wool labeled as merino; assuming this is the truth (not always a given at some fabric stores), it's a very good thing. The merino breed of sheep has been renowned for the softness of its wool since the Middle Ages, and today it's raised solely for its fine, soft fleece. Merino fibers are particularly delicate and smooth (some are even as fine as cashmere) and have antibacterial and moisture-wicking properties—which makes them especially comfortable against the skin, and ideal for anything from finely knit undergarments to athletic apparel. Merino is even warmer than other types of wool, thanks to the air-trapping structure of its fibers. Be forewarned, though, that not all fabrics labeled "merino" are necessarily 100% merino wool. Some synthetics and blends that approximate its uniquely smooth texture might be tagged as merino, so be sure to read labels carefully and ask a salesperson about fiber composition before paying extra for the name.

Above: Wool flannel
Opposite (top to bottom):
Wool gabardine
Wool twill
Wool twill

GABARDINE AND TWILL

Just like their cotton cousins, wool gabardine and twill are marked by diagonal ribs on the surface. Both come in various weights, drape well, resist wrinkling, and are built to last. Wool gabardine—the animal-fiber version of the fabric invented by Thomas Burberry—is often made with worsted wool for a smooth, softly shiny, tailored look. Use both for outerwear (wool's water-resistant quality works in its favor here), as well as tailored and fitted trousers, skirts, and jackets.

(TIP) Gabardine and twill tend to pucker at the seams, especially around curves. Try clipping seam allowances, especially at tricky spots like shoulders and armholes. Use a wool press cloth when pressing, and don't overpress—you can create shiny patches.

WOOL JERSEY
(SEE PHOTO PAGES 88 AND 114)

Though it's technically a knit fabric—and is listed in the Knits chapter—wool jersey, with its soft, sumptuous texture, is a unique, luxurious option for warmth and design drama. Unlike most woven wools, it stretches naturally and lends itself to draping, wrapping, and folding. If you plan on working with it, be sure to follow the sewing tips on page 115.

"**Wool is the cotton of winter. It always had a luxurious connotation, but with new innovations, it's become even more special.**"

—JASON WU

Various wool suiting
fabrics (merino, worsted,
tropical, wool/cashmere)

SUITING AND WORSTED WOOL

After shearing, animal fleece is sorted and cleaned. The longest fibers are combed and spun into **worsted wool**, which is marked by a smooth, lustrous finish that resists snagging and pilling. Worsted wool looks highly polished and is thinner and more flexible than wool fabric made from shorter fibers (a general category called **woolens**), which is why it's ideal for suits and tailored garments worn close to the body.

Fine suiting has information about the yarn thickness woven into the selvage edge. This "S-number" (or "Super S-number") is a gauge of the thickness of the individual wool fibers. The larger the number, the finer the fiber, and the more expensive the fabric. For reference, a nice men's suit might be made of 100s wool; an extremely fine one could be 150s. However, lower S-numbers can still be smooth and lovely; it depends on the finishing.

Suiting comes in a variety of weights appropriate for various climates. Lightweight, comfortable warm-weather suiting is sometimes called **tropical wool**. For suits to be packed for travel, **wool-polyester blends** are especially wrinkle-resistant. Suiting also comes in cashmere and cashmere blends—as fine and luxurious as they sound, and especially warm.

Suiting can be used for things other than suits, of course: trousers, skirts, jackets, and the like. Because it folds and gathers easily, suiting can also be used for draped, shirred, or tailored dresses and gowns. Super-fine suiting is quite pricey, and any sub-par sewing or fit will be obvious. Unless you're an expert, trust a professional tailor to make a custom suit for you. After all, you've already invested in fine fabric!

(TIP) If you are sewing super-fine suiting at home, use thin wool as a press cloth and test-press before heating up the real thing. Before you cut into an expensive textile of any sort, it's a good idea to make a test garment to fine-tune the fit and hone the skills needed for your project. If you're worried, don't be afraid to entrust the job to a professional tailor.

//

TAREK MOHAMMED

Manager, Wool, Mood NYC

Hometown: Bangladesh

Favorite fabric: Cashmere

//

Tarek knows more about wool than just about anyone in the Garment District, but he fell into it by accident. The Bangladesh native moved to New York in the '90s to study computer science, and worked at a Blimpie sandwich shop to support himself. One day in 1997, he came in to visit a friend who worked at Mood, which happened to be hiring. That friend is long gone, but Tarek is still there, now a Mood institution. "I had to learn really fast," he says. "But I fell in love with fabric—it's just as fascinating as computer science."

From his perch in Mood's elegant mahogany-shelved suiting section, Tarek works with United Nations ambassadors, Wall Street tycoons, hip-hop impresarios, New York Knicks players, and visiting dignitaries who seek out Mood's unparalleled selection of fabrics to take back to tailors in their home countries. Tarek also oversees the coating and challis sections of the floor, but it's in suiting where his expertise really shines. "Once you have a custom suit made," he says, "you'll never go back."

"Wool is unique, so modern but so rich in history. Luxurious but functional. After the War, there was nothing but wool, so everything, even wedding dresses, was made from it. I remember my mother sitting up with a pair of huge knitting needles, furiously working away, and in the morning there'd be a new pair of mittens for me."

—VIVIENNE WESTWOOD

Opposite: Assortment of tweeds:

1. Heathered
2. Harris
3. Herringbone
4. Glen plaid (a.k.a Prince of Wales plaid)
5. Donegal
6. Windowpaned (and heathered)
7. Houndstooth

Left: Houndstooth checks aren't just for classic menswear looks. This look from Alexander McQueen's fall/winter 2009 collection utilizes a large-scale version of the pattern and a dramatic silhouette.

TWEED

First used for leisure-class hunting expeditions in the English, Irish, and Scottish countryside because of its water-resistant properties and named for the River Tweed in Scotland, tweed retains an air of gentlemanly, upper-class style. It's a rough, typically unfinished style of woolen fabric that features a variety of textures and colors, notably the **herringbone** version of twill weave as well as **heathered** (variegated) colors, **windowpane checks**, **houndstooth checks**, and **glen plaid**, a.k.a. **Prince of Wales plaid**, a muted pattern of thin grouped rows intersecting to form larger boxes (some of which contain a houndstooth within them). Some specific types of heirloom tweed you might encounter are **Donegal tweed** (named for the county in Ireland where it originates) and **Harris tweed** (woven in the Outer Hebrides of Scotland). These varieties are made the old-fashioned way from local wool and dyed with natural dyes from regional fruits and plants—which is why top designers, eco-minded or not, love to use them for high-quality tailored garments.

(TIPS)

• Most wools are finished for a softer hand. In the case of tweed, the rough, unfinished texture is part of its charm rather than a flaw—but be sure to line tweed garments to avoid uncomfortable itching.

• Thicker versions of tweed are best saved for tailored garments shaped by darts and seams; avoid draping or anything too delicate.

Above:
1. Cashmere
2. Camel hair
3. Rabbit hair blend
4. Mohair
5. Alpaca
6. Cashmere
7. Alpaca

CASHMERE AND EXOTICS

Wools can be made from the hair of animals other than sheep. Cashmere from goats is popular and luxurious, but rabbits, alpacas, vicuñas, and musk oxen also lend their coats to luxurious yarns and fabrics. Often, these pricier fibers are blended with wool from sheep to add a luxurious feel or unique texture.

Costly, rare, and desirable—and once reserved for royalty—**cashmere** is the stuff of legend, and with good reason: It's even softer and warmer than wool (and more expensive). Cashmere's fibers originated from goats in Central Asia, though now the word "cashmere" can apply to any goat fiber 19 microns or smaller in diameter, and goats are raised for cashmere around the world. Even within the cashmere category, there's a hierarchy; the finest cashmeres come from the goats' throats and underbellies, and are extraordinarily soft. Though it's commonly associated with knit sweaters, cashmere comes in a variety of woven options, most notably coating, but in lighter weights it makes for a wonderful splurge for a jacket, pants, or skirt. Cashmere blends offer a more affordable (but still luxurious) option.

Mohair (also called **angora**) comes from goats and has a shaggy, hairy appearance.

Angora rabbit hair, from rabbits and sometimes confused with mohair, often has the same hairy quality. Both are found most often in coating, or in blends to give a fabric more of a textural look and feel. Angora rab-

> "Fabric is the most extraordinary thing, it has life. You must respect the fabric."
>
> —HUBERT DE GIVENCHY

bit hair is the more luxurious and expensive, and is appropriate for people sensitive to the lanolin in wool. It's also warmer than wool.

Real **camel hair** is just that: the undercoat of a camel, renowned for its softness, temperature-regulating properties, and rich honey color. The outer protective fur of a camel is less soft, but often blended with wool. The term "camel hair" is often used to describe any tan or golden wool coating fabric, even if it contains no actual camel hair.

Alpaca is one of Peru's most prominent textile exports and a soft, warm alternative to wool found in everything from coating to sweater knits. The alpaca, a smaller relative of the llama, was specifically bred for its soft fiber, which comes in a plethora of soft, naturally occurring colors. Unlike wool, it does not contain lanolin—a naturally occurring oil—so it's hypoallergenic and ideally suited for those with sensitive skin. Regardless of its softness, alpaca can be itchy against the skin, so be sure to line the fabric with something smooth, like silk habutai.

Vicuña had a moment of pop-culture fame in David Lynch's *Twin Peaks* series when a very well-dressed would-be murderer was nabbed via the fibers of her vicuña coat that were left behind at the scene of the crime. (No one else in town had the means to buy such a luxurious item.) Yes, vicuña—so named for the national animal of Peru, a relative of the llama—is expensive. So much so, in fact, that it was the fabric of Incan royalty. Nowadays, "when you do find vicuña, it's probably going

to be a blend," according to Mood's Tarek Mohammed. Each animal produces only half a kilogram of wool per year, but it's one of the finest wools in the world at an average of 12 micrometers in fiber diameter—even finer than most cashmere. (A 100% vicuña coat will probably cost in the five figures.)

(TIPS)

- A walking presser foot will keep things running smoothly at the sewing machine, especially if your fabric has a nap.

- If the fabric does have a nap, be sure to cut all pieces with the nap facing the same way, and sew in the direction of the nap, not against it.

- Use a silk organza press cloth when pressing these fabrics.

- Use only the point of a steam iron—called *point pressing* or *couture pressing*—to avoid leaving indentations in the fabric.

- Clip seam allowances along curved areas to prevent bunching.

- If you're a beginning sewer, consider sending your pattern and fabric to a professional tailor.

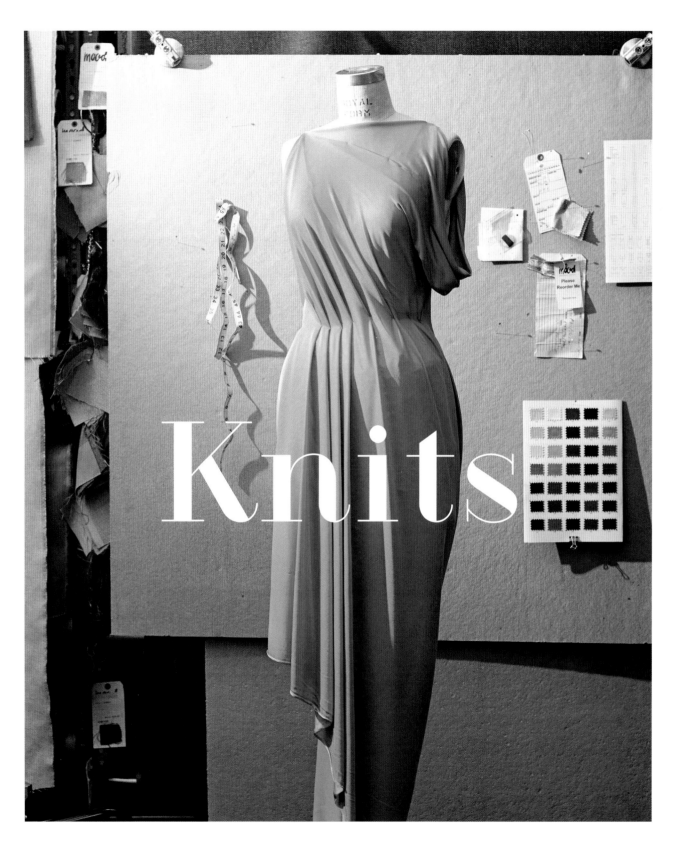

Knits

WOVENS AND KNITS ARE apples and oranges. You can walk into a fabric store not knowing exactly what you want to fabricate your garment with, but one thing you have to be sure of is whether your pattern requires a woven or a knit. Occasionally one can be switched for the other, but for most purposes, it's one *or* the other.

Knit fabrics are formed from interlocking loops of yarn, and all have some degree of natural stretch, which is why the process of designing and sewing with them is totally different than it is for wovens, where most beginners start. But that's no reason to be intimidated. Knit fabrics are comfortable, soft, and accommodating to the body's curves and movements; they can be as casual as your favorite cotton T-shirt, as elegant as a silk jersey goddess gown, or as structured as a chic, tailored ponte di roma jacket. Once you have each knit's unique rules of sewing down pat, you'll want to whip up an entire wardrobe with them.

Knits can be divided into two categories: **stable** (fabrics that retain their shape relatively well and stretch relatively little) and **unstable** (fabrics that can stretch far beyond their original size). Knits' instability sometimes has to do with the inclusion of stretch fiber, like spandex (often called by its trade name Lycra), although loosely knit fabrics also have unstable properties. Loose knits are the trickiest to work with, and sometimes respond to patterns differently than do stable, structured knits (that is, they might look bigger when finished, if they don't have

good recovery). Both, however, should be carefully controlled during sewing and gently fed into the machine so that they don't stretch out at the seams. Read on for more advice about how to work with these versatile, easy-to-wear fabrics.

SEWING KNIT FABRICS

SPLURGE ON A SERGER. The pros use this specialty machine, which trims the seam allowance, sews a stretch seam, and encloses the seam allowance with multiple spools of thread, all in one fell swoop. If you don't have a serger and aren't ready to invest in one, you can use a regular sewing machine with stretch stitch or a narrow zigzag stitch—consult your machine's manual to get the setting right—but whatever you do, don't use a regular straight stitch; its failure to stretch will not only likely look uneven, but quickly cause stitches to break. The best option is to buy a **twin needle** (which requires two spools of thread) and use it with a **zigzag foot**; this will create two rows of straight stitching on the upper layer, with a zigzag beneath, and will make stretch fabric easier to sew. Otherwise, a simple stretch stitch or narrow zigzag stitch will do the trick.

MIND YOUR HEMS. If you'll be sewing knits often, you might also want to invest in a **coverstitch/chainstitch machine** to finish hems with ease. This creates a professional-looking double row of stitching at the hem. If you don't have one, worry not; simply sew your hems with a double-needle, stretch, or narrow zigzag stitch. If the hem of your garment is so big that it's unlikely to be stretched and stressed—as in a voluminous skirt or oversized tee—a straight stitch might be okay. In the case of jersey, you can also leave hems raw; they won't ravel, and they are likely to curl up with some cross-grain tugging, which actually looks like a finish of sorts. Note that some top-of-the-line sergers (those listed as using five or more threads) include a coverstitch, so you can have both functions in one machine. However, the conversion process from regular serging to coverstitching can be tedious, with adding attachments and rethreading the machine; some sewers find it easier to purchase both machines.

GET TO THE (BALL) POINT. Ball-point needles are designed to be used with knit fabrics. They prevent ripping and tearing—especially important if you'll be using a delicate knit. If not, as in the case of thick fleece or double knit, you might be able to get away with a universal needle. For highly elastic knits, especially those with spandex, try a stretch needle, which is a modified ball-point type. It's helpful in preventing skipped stitches.

USE SYNTHETIC THREAD. Polyester, rather than cotton or silk, is ideal for stretch fabrics; it's the least likely to snap and break. **Wooly nylon thread** is another option; it's a thread that actually stretches, and is specifically designed for use with knits. It's really intended for a serger, but you can also use it on the bobbin of a sewing machine (but not in the needle, where it will snag). If you

"The wrap dress was an interesting cultural phenomenon, and one that has lasted 30 years. What is so special about it is that it's actually a very traditional form of clothing. It's like a toga, it's like a kimono, without buttons, without a zipper. What made my wrap dresses different is that they were made out of jersey and they sculpted the body."

—DIANE VON FURSTENBERG

Above: Diane von Furstenberg's wrap dress was an instant success in the 1970s and remains a classic today. Jersey makes the silhouette comfortable, easy to care for, and flattering to the body.

do this, you'll need to hand-wind the bobbin. The primary downside to wooly nylon is that it doesn't come in as many colors as regular thread and it's tricky in conventional machines.

USE A WALKING FOOT. A walking presser foot (a.k.a. even-feed foot) allows both layers of fabric to slide evenly along during sewing—especially important with stretch fabrics, which can stretch out of shape when they stick to the presser foot. This can make a huge difference in the quality and straightness of your seams and prevent unsightly rippling caused by too much stretching.

WE'LL SAY IT AGAIN: WATCH OUT FOR STRETCHING DURING SEWING. There's an art to doing this; you've got to feed the fabric at just the right speed, taking care not to let it pull in any one direction, or stitches and seams will be weak and stretched-out. You might want to sandwich pattern pieces between tissue paper to keep the feed dogs from eating up the fabric, or use stabilizing paper tape to be torn away. Which combination of techniques and accessories is best for your specific fabric? Practice, practice, practice on test swatches first to find out.

DON'T PIN INTO THE BODY OF A GARMENT DURING THE LAYING OUT AND CUTTING OF PATTERN PIECES. This is a Mood rule for almost every type of fabric, but it's worth repeating in the case of knit fabrics. A hole in your knit fabric will not heal itself; it will only get bigger, or cause an unsightly, unfixable run.

> "We can fit clothes more snugly so women can move as freely as if they had nothing on."
>
> —DONNA KARAN

IF YOU USE INTERFACING, CHOOSE ONE WITH STRETCH. This may sound like a no-brainer, but you'd be surprised how many experienced sewers make this rookie mistake. Interfacing can be a great tool for stabilizing high-stress areas and stretch seams, but be sure it stretches with the fabric—look for a lightweight tricot version, and cut it along the same grain as the pattern piece where it will be attached. Mood doesn't recommend fusible interfacing for knits, as it will peel right off (unevenly and unattractively) as the fabric stretches.

GET TO KNOW STRETCH SEAM-STABILIZING TAPE. Available in clear silicone elastic and tricot varieties, this tape will stay in your seam (rather than tearing out, as with paper stabilizing tape) and will keep high-stress, weight-bearing areas—notably shoulder seams—from stretching out and ripping apart once the garment is finished.

CARING FOR KNIT FABRICS

Consult the rules for each fabric composition. If you're working with cotton jersey, for instance, be sure to preshrink. Silk jersey requires delicate handling and pressing, while rayon or polyester jersey should be kept away from direct heat to prevent melting or permanent marking. In general, avoid the machine dryer unless, as with cotton knits, you've thoroughly preshrunk your fabric and have sewn it together sturdily. Once your garment is sewn, consider storing it in a drawer rather than on a hanger to keep it from stretching out, especially if it's made from a heavy, unstable, or loose-knit fabric.

The following knit fabrics are grouped by structure or function, but within some of the categories, you'll find a broad range of variation—starting with the very fiber itself. A jersey knit fabric, for instance, might be made of cotton or silk or rayon or a blend of several fibers; it could be stable or unstable, sheer or substantial, stretchy or less so.

JERSEY

The most common knit fabric, jersey is a single-knit, flat, light- to medium-weight fabric that usually has a modest amount of stretch. The right side is smooth, with grainwise "courses" of V-shaped knit stitches, while the wrong side shows cross-grain loops—the purl stitches of the knit. Jersey comes in just about any variety, from stiff cotton to cozy wool to slinky silk and smooth cellulose fibers like lyocell (Tencel) and bamboo rayon. (Many activewear fabrics are also jersey knits; see page 122 for more details.) These days, many jersey knits include a small percentage (2% to 10%) of spandex, to strengthen the fabric and, more importantly, to improve its recovery after stretching. The spandex doesn't appreciably change the hand of the fabric, but it does reduce the tendency of knits to sag or bag with wear.

Different varieties drape differently, but all are useful for T-shirts! Depending on the weight and opacity, you might use jersey for anything from a scarf (just cut a rectangle) to leggings to a draped, shirred dress. What distinguishes jersey from other types of knit fabrics is the way it rolls. The cut edge curls up toward the face; this is how you know which side is the face (though some designers like to work with the wrong side facing out, too; with patterns like stripes, it can provide a more textured, softer look). Sometimes, this curled edge can be a design element, as in a raw dress hem or neck binding.

Fine jersey, as a category, refers to jersey that is delicate and sometimes slightly sheer. **Microfiber jerseys**, made with micro-sized fibers, also fall into this category. Fine jerseys drape and gather especially beautifully and feel like heaven against the skin, but are slippery and difficult to work with, and often expensive (but they look it).

(TIPS)

- Fine jersey hems look lovely left raw. Just beware—they curl more than other jerseys, so leave extra seam-allowance space.

- Avoid using fine jersey for any styles that might require interfacing or notions, such as plackets with buttons or zippers. Fine jersey simply isn't sturdy enough to withstand the stress! T-shirts, tanks, pull-on skirts, or draped styles—anything without closures such as zippers and buttons—are your best bet.

Above: Jersey fabrics
1. Silk
2. Rayon
3. Ultrafine silk
4. Modal
5. Matte
6. Wool
7. Bamboo
8. Cotton
9. Tricot
10. Microfiber

- For ultrathin, delicate jerseys, use the thinnest ball-point needle you can get your hands on (such as 60/8).
- Use stretch stabilizing tape on shoulders and other stretch-prone areas.
- Use tissue paper between the fabric and feed dogs to provide stability during sewing.
- Test thread tension on scraps and troubleshoot before you sew.

Silk jersey is super-slippery—beginners beware! It has a luxurious sheen and dramatic, fluid drape that lends a soigné glamour to draped, shirred, or voluminous dresses, tops, and jumpsuits.

(TIPS)

- Follow the care rules for silk when using silk jersey, and take extra care when pressing and cutting to prevent damage to the fabric from heat or pins.
- Use stabilizing tape to keep seams in line during sewing.
- Don't let slippery, fluid silk jersey hang off the table while you're cutting or sewing—keep it level to avoid pulling during sewing.
- As with fine jersey, test thread tension on a scrap before taking on your pattern pieces.

Bamboo/Tencel/Modal jersey are new eco-alternatives made with cellulosic fibers obtained through a viscose process, meaning that they're similar to rayon jersey—though they can also feel a lot like cotton. **Bamboo**, also called **bamboo rayon**, is derived from the fast-growing bamboo plant; **Tencel** comes from eucalyptus pulp (see page 26). **Modal** and **micromodal** come from beech tree pulp. Some are extremely soft and fine, especially micro modal, which is popular for intimates and delicate, high-end scarves.

(TIP) Take care to preshrink these jerseys as you would cotton.

Even the roughest bast fibers can be knitted into jersey. **Linen and hemp jerseys** are popular T-shirt alternatives in contemporary fashion because of the slubbed effect they often feature. Unevenly textured bumps lend depth and texture to what is typically a flat surface. Some linen and hemp jerseys are semi-sheer; try combining different layers in a garment, or plan your underpinnings accordingly.

Rayon—the traditional viscose fiber—can be spun into all sorts of jerseys. Some are inexpensive, found in the lower end of the casual-wear market, and tend to pill with wear and washing. Others have a cotton-like, almost fuzzy softness. Another type of rayon jersey you might find is what designers call **matte jersey**. This has all the dramatic drape of silk jersey, but none of the sheen, and is beautifully opaque and heavy. High-end designers rely on it for sleek dresses, sexy tops, and fluid trousers; it behaves best when dry-cleaned.

Wool jersey is a beautiful, high-end fabric that can be thick and warm or delicate and sheer. It makes for great cut-and-sew sweaters or cool-weather layering pieces, such as long-sleeved tops or simple pull-on skirts. However, it's not an easy-care, wash-and-wear fabric like, say, cotton jersey; as with woven wool fabrics, you can't wash it in the machine (unless you are trying to make **felted wool**). Wool jerseys also tend not to come with stretch blended in, so avoid using styles that require recovery to keep their shape, such as close-fitting pants (which will bag out at the knees and rear).

Opposite:
1. Double knit
2–3. Interlock
4. Ponte di roma

TRICOT

This term technically refers to a style of knitting, but for fabric purposes, it refers to an
old-school, closely knitted type of fabric that
doesn't stretch—think retro brassieres and
slips, or stiff cotton vintage sweaters. Though
it's fallen out of favor as a fashion fabric, tricot makes a great interfacing or lining for less
stable knits.

DOUBLE KNIT

This term refers to a heavier-weight, more
stable and substantial type of knit fabric,
formed with two layers for a double-faced
versatility. Double knit is used for more tailored garments, like jackets, structured tops
and dresses, and pants. It doesn't stretch
much (unless it contains stretch fiber), but
generally retains its shape and structure
beautifully, and is easy for beginners to work
with because it won't slip and slide around.

INTERLOCK

Interlock is a common knit fabric that's more
substantial, and easier to work with, than jersey. (Think of the turtlenecks you wore as a
child.) Its interlocking knit structure makes
it double-faced, opaque, and very stable, and
in fact, it is a type of double knit. It can form
anything from dresses to tops to bottoms.
However, that very stability means it's not
always the best choice for garments that
need to do a ton of stretching (unless it contains stretch fiber).

(TIP) Unlike jersey, interlock doesn't roll, so
you'll want to finish your hems.

PONTE DI ROMA

Ponte di roma is a type of double knit—
meaning it has all the structure and stability
(and ease of sewing) of this type of fabric.
Substantial, sturdy, and often blended with a
touch of stretch fiber, ponte di roma provides
both structure and compression, making it
ideal for styles both sculptural (dramatic
peplums and oversized silhouettes) and skin-
tight (fitted pencil skirts and dresses, slim
pants). Ponte (as it's known for short) has
a solid, expensive look, and smooths away
imperfections in the body—which is why so
many ready-to-wear designers (and the Kar-
dashian sisters) love it. It sometimes comes
in prints, which are the only type of ponte
that might not look the same on both sides.
The name means "Roman bridge," which may
refer to the structure of loops that bind the
two layers together.

RIB KNIT
(SEE PHOTO PAGE 108)

Distinguished by its vertical lines, rib knit
fabric expands and contracts like crazy, which
is why you'll find it used to finish areas that
need to be stretched, like neck and sleeve
openings. Because it can grow so much, it's
also a popular choice for garments and accessories that are meant to be skin-tight, like
fitted tanks, legwarmers, and hats.

DATE	YDS	STYLE	C/T	BAL
2/4/14	1 yard			11 $\frac{5}{8}$

FLEECE

Fleece is usually a knit fabric, though it can sometimes be woven, and it may be hard to tell the difference. Distinguished by a soft, fuzzy nap on both sides, it's one of the easiest and most fun fabrics to work with, and it feels soft and cuddly. Though it's usually reserved for loungewear, robes, infant and children's wear, and technical sports outerwear (rather than fashion-forward styles), fleece can be a fresh, interesting, and ultra cozy alternative to sweatshirt fabric or French terry for sweaters, sweatshirts, pants, and even skirts and dresses. Traditional **wool fleece** has the same soft, fuzzy nap as polar fleece, though it's more expensive and harder to come by. **Polar fleece** is a catchall term for synthetic (usually polyester) fleece, found in everything from slippers to pajamas. **Technical fleece** is the sort of advanced athletic fleece you'll find in a Patagonia store; it can be embossed, bonded, or specially treated in numerous ways for warmth, windproofing, and moisture-wicking properties.

(TIPS)

• Fleece can be bulky when folded. Use it for simpler styles (not elaborate folds), and finish seams with binding, a serger, or an overlock stitch. Or just leave them raw; fleece won't ravel.

• Fleece is likely to leave fuzz all over your sewing area. Clean your machine after each use, and have a tape lint roller handy.

DESIGN TIP
Use sweatshirt fleece as you would French terry, but use the fuzzy side on the outside sparingly—it tends to pill, pill, and pill some more, and is best kept against the skin, where it feels soft and warm.

DESIGN TIP
The back side of French terry isn't necessarily the wrong side. Use the looped side as a contrasting element on pockets, plackets, waistbands, or yokes—or make a sweatshirt with the looped side out.

SWEATSHIRT FLEECE

Not to be confused with polar (polyester) or wool **fleece**, **sweatshirt fleece** functions the same way as French terry: It has a smooth side and a fuzzy, napped side (instead of loops). Sweatshirt fleece tends to be quite stable rather than loose-knit, and to curl up at the edges, meaning that hems can be left raw for an edgy look. It's perfect for sweats as well as cozy takes on everyday silhouettes like jackets, tops, and dresses.

TERRY CLOTH AND FRENCH TERRY

Terry is for far more than bath towels. It's a type of fabric that has loops on both sides. It can be knit or woven: The fabric that forms your bath towels is woven, for instance, but many sewers like to work with knit terry to make fun, stretchy styles, such as beach cover-ups, loungewear, and athletic sweatbands. Stretch terries tend to come in fun colors and even prints. **French terry** is an incredibly versatile variant with one smooth side and one looped side. It can be very stable or very unstable, depending on the knit; it can be 100% cotton or rayon or even bamboo rayon; it can have flat, thin loops or big, chunky ones; the loops can be the same color as the right side, or a contrast color. Designers love to use French terry for sweatshirts, hoodies, sweatpants, and more elevated staples like jackets and skirts.

Above (top to bottom):
Polar fleece
Technical fleece
French terry
Polyester fleece
Polyester fleece
Terry cloth
Polyester fleece
Waffle knit
French terry
Wool fleece
Sweatshirt fleece

(TIPS)

- The loops of these fabrics fray and shed a lot. Keep a lint roller handy!
- Terry fabrics have a nap, especially those with looser loops. Take care to keep pattern pieces facing the same direction.
- Use a longer stitch length to accommodate the fabric's bulk, especially for thicker terries. Consider using a contrast-color thread so that you can spot your stitches more easily.
- Edges must be enclosed, or else the seams will continue to shed. Try finishing seams with a serger, or enclose them with a stretch binding of cross-grain strips of knit fabric.

WAFFLE KNIT

Distinguished by its three-dimensional square-patterned surface, waffle-knit fabric is especially good at retaining heat, which is why it's most often used for long johns and classic thermal tops. You might also try it as an alternative to jersey or fleece for other types of casual clothing and cozy loungewear (tees, hoodies, robes, pants, and the like). Its rich texture could also add a nice element of depth to a more polished silhouette, like a knit dress or jacket. (Note: Waffle knit is not to be confused with **waffle weave** fabric, which is, you guessed it, woven instead of knit. Waffle weave tends to be very chunky, and is more likely to be used for robes, blankets, or towels than for apparel.)

1. Open work sweater knit
2. Acrylic/modacrylic knit
3. Pointelle
4. Sweater knit

ACRYLIC was invented as an alternative to wool in the 1940s and is derived from petroleum byproducts. It can also mimic the textures of cotton and silk. Today, many sweater knits that look and feel like wool are either a wool-acrylic blend, or even 100% synthetic. Acrylic is lighter in weight than animal hair—which can be a big advantage in bulky styles like fisherman sweaters—but unlike animal hair, it is flammable, so keep it away from heat and irons.

MODACRYLIC is similar to acrylic (the differences are on a molecular level) but nonflammable. Both can be prone to pilling, though some types have been treated to prevent this. Both are also prone to generating static electricity. Although they may be thought of as "cheap" because they are synthetic substitutes for natural fibers and can be scratchy, some acrylic knits and blends can be quite elegant in texture and hand. Let your fingertips be the judge.

POINTELLE

Many of the **sweater-knit fabrics** at Mood are **pointelle knits**—so named for a knit technique that creates open work patterns on the surface. (Some pointelle knits, however, aren't sweater knits—they can function more like regular T-shirt jersey fabric, but with tiny holes.) Pointelle has a sweet, romantic feeling that makes it perfect for loungewear, dresses, and girls' clothes, as well as all sorts of sweaters and tops. If the open patterns will be worn over any not-for-public-display areas of the body, however, line the garment or wear something underneath.

SWEATER KNITS

What's the difference between knit fabrics and the knit material that composes sweaters? Well, sweaters usually aren't made from fabric, but rather from specially shaped knitted panels that are **linked** (that is, knitted or sewn) together. However, there are plenty of **sweater-knit fabrics** at Mood and other stores that have the look and feel of sweaters—but are sold on the roll or bolt so that you can cut and sew them as you would other fabric to make your own sweaters (or dresses, or scarves, or hats) instead of whipping out your knitting needles. Sweater-knit fabrics aren't your standard jerseys or terries; they can be chunky or fine, with open work or solid and textured, but what sets them apart are their specialty textures and thicknesses. In other words, they look like sweaters!

(TIPS)

• Sweater knits distort during stitching; cut them with extra-wide seam allowances (¾" to 1" [2 cm to 2.5 cm]), and trim the excess after sewing.

• Sweater knits will begin raveling the moment you cut them. Use a serger to sew them if at all possible. If you don't have one, use a wide zigzag stitch and trim close to the edge, or else enclose seam or hem edges with a stretch binding.

• Invest in a walking foot to keep friction-prone sweater knits moving smoothly through your sewing machine.

• Gently feed the fabric through the machine so it doesn't stretch. This is important with all knit fabrics, but especially sweater knits.

• Stabilize seams that might stretch during wear, such as shoulder seams, with seam stabilizing tape.

Above: A sweater dress on Halston's fall 1973 ready-to-wear runway. Sweater knits can be both chic and cozy.

ACTIVEWEAR KNIT FABRICS

Activewear fabric isn't just for the gym. This category spans a broad range of styles, including everything from technical waffle knits, mesh, spandex interlocks, and specialty jersey blends such as SeaCell (a type of lyocell, made from seaweed cellulose, that feels cool against the skin). What differentiates activewear fabrics from their non-technical counterparts? Activewear knit fabrics are often made primarily of synthetic fiber; they stretch and recover especially well; and they sometimes have special properties, such as moisture wicking. While all of these fabrics are designed to accommodate the body as it moves and sweats, they can be a fun, sporty choice when used for everyday garments like jackets and dresses.

(TIPS)

- Wooly nylon thread feels softer and more comfortable for garments that will rub against the skin.
- If you have a serger or overlock machine, consider using **flatlock seams** for activewear (see right). These seams contain the seam allowances within a column of overlock stitching and holds them flat against the fabric, to reduce the potential for loose seam allowances to chafe the skin.
- Finish edges with a coverstitch, twin- needle hem, or with a binding cut on the crossgrain from fabric with an equal amount of stretch, and applied with a zigzag stitch.

MESH

This holey fabric comes in various weights and degrees of stretch. **Athletic mesh**, used for sports jerseys and outdoor gear, is thick, tough, and non-stretchy; **power mesh** is stretchy but strong; **illusion mesh** is much finer, stretches a lot, and is often combined with other knit fabrics to create sheer panels that appear as nude skin. In recent years, mesh has come out of the locker room and onto the runways, becoming an interesting

Avoid having seam allowances rub against your skin as you work out by using one of these methods. You can use either of these methods decoratively as well, by choosing contrasting thread.

SERGED FLATLOCK SEAM: Set your serger for a three-thread overlock stitch. Adjust the thread tensions so the needle thread has no tension (a setting of zero), the upper looper has a normal setting, and the lower looper is tightened slightly, to a setting of about seven. Make test seams to fine-tune the tension settings.

With wrong sides together, serge the seam. Then, open the fabric layers, pulling apart gently. The seam allowances will either flatten and overlap within the stitching column, or fold slightly into a flat configuration.

ZIGZAG-COMBO MOCK FLATLOCK: Trim seam allowances to ¼" (6 mm) wide. Set your sewing machine for a narrow zigzag stitch. With wrong sides together, sew the seam. Finger-press the seam allowances together and to one side (usually toward the center or back of the garment). Set the machine for a wide zigzag (4 mm) and top-stitch over the seam allowances to anchor them to the garment's surface. Be sure the stitch covers and secures the raw edges of the allowances.

alternative for shirts, dresses, and contrast pieces like pockets and sleeves. It also looks cool when layered, forming eye-dazzling circular patterns. Keep modesty in mind, and line mesh garments or wear something underneath.

Tulle is a type of mesh, but it is woven and not knitted and used for very different applications than knit mesh. See the Silks chapter for more about tulle.

(TIPS)

- Much of mesh's surface is air; use stretch stabilizing tape to support seams when sewing.
- Use tissue paper between fabric and feed dogs; you can tear this away after sewing.
- When stitching mesh to another fabric, work with the mesh on top.
- Consider finishing raw edges with binding; it's the cleanest option, and edges will show through because of fabric's transparency.

SWIMWEAR FABRIC

Part of the activewear category, ultrastretchy swimwear fabric is generally made with synthetic fibers, which stand up best to salt water and chlorine. It will always include stretch fiber, such as spandex, to accommodate movements. (Sometimes this type of fabric itself is casually referred to as **spandex**.) Because it's so flexible, swimwear fabric is also great for outside-the-pool uses like dancewear, costumes, leggings, and accessories that need to stretch, like workout headbands. You can also use it for swim cover-ups, of course!

(TIPS)

- If at all possible, use a serger to sew swimwear. A stretch or zigzag stitch can work, but a serged finish is the most durable.
- If using a regular sewing machine, install a stretch needle to prevent skipped stitches.
- Swimwear should be lined with special swimwear lining fabric for modesty and comfort. This is generally sold alongside the swimwear fabric. When purchasing elastic, be sure to look for a product that's labeled safe for swimwear; it can withstand chlorine, salt water, sunblock chemicals, and the heat of hot tubs.
- For waistbands, leg openings, and other high-stress areas, consider inserting clear elastic along the seam. This both makes the fabric easier to sew and helps these fit-intensive areas hold their shape.
- Try sandwiching the fabric between tissue paper to prevent stretching out during sewing.

Silks

T HE FIRST THING YOU'LL see when you walk in the door at Mood's New York City store? Silk, silk, and more silk. From the front to the back along several aisles, intricate brocades, wispy chiffons, and sumptuous four-plies are packed in ceiling-high. Upright bins near the front door heave with printed crepes and embellished velvets straight from the runways of Marc Jacobs, J. Mendel, and Carolina Herrera. Not surprisingly, some shoppers get so taken with Mood's silks that they never even make it upstairs to the wool department.

The rich history of silk only adds to its appeal. Legend has it that the chief wife of Emperor Huang Ti (2677-2597 B.C.) discovered silk when a cocoon dropped from a tree into her cup of tea, and Lady Hsi-Ling drew out a long thread. The Chinese maintained a monopoly on silk production for thousands of years, exporting to the Middle East and Europe via the legendary Silk Road, a route through which languages, cultures, and cuisines also intermingled. It wasn't until the time of the Crusades that Italy became known for its sericulture (silk production), with France following closely behind. Today China is once again the largest producer of silk, though Mood also continues to source fine silk from India, Korea, Thailand, and Vietnam.

Though silk was for centuries a luxury fabric—during the first millennium of its use in China, it was reserved solely for use by emperors and dignitaries—it has become fairly ubiquitous since the advent of mass fashion, and some of it is priced quite accessi-bly. Silk feels cool to wear in the summer yet warm in the winter, and nothing moves more dramatically (whether smooth and fluid or stiff and structured) or feels better against the skin. Designers and *Project Runway* contestants can't get enough of it.

The only downside to silk (besides its generally higher price per yard) is that the same qualities that make it so alluring also make it a slippery devil to cut and sew. (All but the most intrepid of beginners should probably get comfortable with cotton first.) This chapter addresses the most common cutting and sewing conundrums for silk and how to prevent them. With patience and preparation, the styles you sew in silk can look and feel perfectly professional.

SEWING SILK FABRICS

WEIGHT, DON'T PIN. Treat yourself to a pair of iron pattern weights like the professionals use. Garment District pattern cutters don't use pins to hold down patterns. These old pros think that pinning patterns is too time-consuming; it's also less accurate, because you're only securing the edges of the pattern. In other words, you'd never pin the body of a pattern piece (the pinhole would be permanent), but the center of your pattern piece can shift while cutting. Heavy weights used throughout the pattern piece will keep all fabrics, and especially slippery fabrics like silks, securely in place during cutting. Professionals simply move these weights around on the pattern as they cut. You can also make do with heavy washers from the hardware

Previous pages: Left to right: Silk habutai (China silk); silk charmeuse dress draped by Juan Carlos Rios Negron.

store, or you can get creative and wrap bricks in fabric. (Some sewers use cans from the kitchen pantry as weights, but inspect them carefully before use. One of Mood's employees had a can leach right through the pattern paper and imprint a ring onto the satin of what was to be a jacket.)

PINS ARE OKAY—SOMETIMES. Pins alone aren't ideal for silk, but they have their place. If your silk is especially shifty, pin it in a single layer to tissue paper or other lightweight plain paper before cutting. Place the pins around the edges and in areas between where the pattern pieces will be cut—not on the pattern pieces! Then place your pattern pieces on top of the silk-paper layers, add weights, cut, and remove the paper.

USE THE RIGHT NEEDLE. This is a mandate for all fabrics, but especially so for silks. Test results with a 60/8 needle and polyester thread; there's no need to use expensive silk thread. A Microtex needle may work well, but Mood's team often gets equally good results with Universal needles. Generally, more delicate fabrics require more delicate needles.

PRESS FOR SUCCESS. The hallmark of a well-made garment is in the pressing, and this holds true for silk. Always use a press cloth on top of the silk, and test your iron's heat levels on a scrap first, since too-high heat can scorch delicate silks. The Mood team is partial to silk organza as press cloth, because it's transparent and withstands high heat. Try taking a yard of white or other light-colored silk organza, cutting it into 12" (30-cm) or

so squares, and then serge or pink the edges. If your iron spits or drips water, empty the water out completely and use a dry iron: Don't risk water spots. Press your seams flat first to meld the stitches into your silk, then press the allowances open. To prevent show-through ridges from appearing on the right side of the fabric when pressing seams open, use a wooden seam-stick pressing tool.

TEST EVERYTHING FIRST. This includes needle size, stitch length, pressing, and marking. Working with a large scrap of your silk, make sure your marking method completely disappears on a scrap before you try it on your garment; plain old chalk may be your best bet.

PLAN SEAM FINISHES AHEAD. French seams work well on straight seams and on lightweight silks. You can also hand-overcast silk

Above: From the pages of *Vogue*, December 1945. Silk has long been the fabric of choice for dramatic evening looks.

DESIGN TIP
If you can't control silk as you sew, the seams will appear wavy. To prevent this from happening, cut 2"- (5-cm-) wide strips of parchment paper or pattern paper totaling the length of your seams. Place the fabric right sides together and pin the seam allowances to the paper strips. Stitch, with the paper layer on the bottom. Gently tear away the paper. Adding this paper layer stabilizes the silk and improves sewing results.

seams; on four-ply silk we've pressed open, stitched close to the edge of the seam, then pinked the edges. Proceed with caution before serging or zigzagging on lighter-weight silks, as the thread can pull too tightly and scrunch the edge of the seam allowance.

SILK THREAD NOT REQUIRED. Regular polyester thread works fine; save silk thread for hand-basting, as it's less likely to mar silk and is easier to remove. That said, fine silk thread is sometimes an excellent choice when sewing very lightweight silks; it creates virtually no bulk in narrow seams and hems.

HAPPY ENDINGS, AND BEGINNINGS. Silk's delicate nature makes it less likely than other fabrics to stay put during sewing. Here's a trick: Begin your seam on a small strip of paper that overlaps the silk and continue sewing onto the fabric. When you're done, tear away the paper and knot the thread ends together. Never backstitch to secure a seam; just clip threads and tie a knot.

PIN OR BASTE CAREFULLY. Watch how you hold your pattern pieces together when sewing seams. If you pin, do so in the seams, where the holes the pins create won't show.

WALK THE WALK. Use a walking foot to keep it all together. The walking foot's purpose is to keep the two layers of fabric together as they feed through your machine, combatting the differential feed inherent in almost all sewing machines (the fabric closest to the feed dogs passes through the needle slightly ahead of the layer on top). Silks play much nicer when you use a walking foot.

> **"Cash register tape is perfect for stabilizing silk seams."**
> —KENNETH D. KING

INTERFACE WITH CARE. No matter how addicted you are to fusible interfacings, don't even think about using one on your silk garment until you test a piece on a scrap first. Some fusibles may cause bubbling of the fabric, which ruins its look and feel. Mood's staff is partial to sew-in interfacings, especially for silks. When shopping, take your main silk fabric and pair it with different types of lightweight wovens—silk organza, silk voile, cotton batiste, and cotton flannelette, for example—to see which best provides the support and structure your garment needs.

AVOID TENSION HEADACHES. Test your machine tension on a scrap. Always make sure the tension on your machine isn't too tight, or it will cause your silk to pull and pucker.

CARING FOR SILK FABRICS

Machine-washing silk fabric can transform it from smooth and sleek to rough and ratty. If you want your silk fabric to look as fine as it does on the bolt—pure and untouched—Mood recommends leaving the care of your silk garments to the dry cleaner. A trustworthy dry cleaner can often make your sewn garments look even better, because they can press and steam more effectively and precisely.

However, some silks can be safely washed by hand or in your machine on the super-delicate cycle. Other silks, such as sturdier crepes and habutais, can actually soften nicely after gentle washing (provided the garment itself isn't too intricate for the washing machine). Try washing a swatch before you cut out your pattern.

Silk comes in a seemingly endless array of weights, textures, and styles. Choosing the right one for your project depends on the function of the garment, the type of texture and drape you're after, and your comfort level (because some types are easier to sew than others). Below is a guide to the major varieties of silk fabric, organized by dominant characteristics, such as weight, drape, hand, and surface texture. You'll find shiny, sheer, soft, crisp, and fancy varieties like velvet and brocade. For each type of silk, we've addressed its key properties, popular uses, and specific tips helpful for handling and sewing it.

TUTORIAL: GELATIN WASH PRETREATMENT FOR CHARMEUSE

Try this trick used by Paris couture houses to firm up slippery charmeuse to make it easier to sew. Let sheets of fabric soak for an hour in a solution of 1 teaspoon gelatin powder (available at any grocery store) to every 2 cups water (or, depending on how much you have, just use the entire packet in the bathtub). Drain the tub, roll the fabric gently inside a towel to remove excess water, and air-dry. After cutting and sewing, carefully wash the garment in warm, soapy water, rinse and air-dry, and voilà! The gelatin is gone, and the silk's slippery quality returns.

Above: Jean Harlow in a dress by Adrian, 1935. Shiny silk charmeuse has a screen-siren glamour to it.

CHARMEUSE
(SEE PHOTO PAGE 130)

Seductive and slinky, the favored fabric of 1930s screen sirens—and designers of sumptuous lingerie—charmeuse is a light-weight, softly draping fabric that clings to the body. It demands attention when worn, and patience when sewn. But it makes for especially alluring eveningwear and intimates (try it with bias-cut patterns), and can be a luxurious lining fabric. Charmeuse has a satin side and a matte side, and either works as the right side in a garment: Though the satin side has an appealing sheen, using it on the inside creates a slippery, luxurious feeling against the skin. The Mood team always prefers silk charmeuse over polyester charmeuse, which tends to fray like crazy during cutting and handling.

SATIN

Customers often ask the team at Mood about "regular satins" and are momentarily befuddled when we ask them what type of satin they're looking for: Duchesse satin? Crepe-backed satin? Double-faced satin? And would you like that in silk, viscose, or polyester? "Satin" is really an adjective, and refers to the smooth, lustrous appearance obtained by a weave of long floating yarns in the warp. Lightweight satins can work for tops, loosely structured jackets, and lingerie, while the heavier weights are most often used in eveningwear and bridal designs. Double-faced satin and satin-backed crepe (or crepe-backed satin) offer two textures in one for styles in which the wrong side (or inside feel) is as important as the right side. As with many other types of fabric, in the case of satin, Mood's team is, of course, partial to silk over synthetics. Polyester satin tends to be stiffer, sweatier, and less elegant.

(TIPS)

- Pins leave holes in the finely woven surface of satin fabrics, so only pin in the seam allowances or in other areas where marks won't show.
- Satin's long floating yarns are snag-prone. Always start your satin project with a new, sharp needle that's appropriate for the weight of your fabric. Change your needle at the first sign of dullness because snags can ruin a garment's appearance. And handle the garment with care at all times. Even dry hands or a not-quite-smooth fingernail can snag satin.

DUCHESSE SATIN

As its name suggests, duchesse satin has a regal quality. It has a satiny sheen on one side (the other is matte), it comes in substantial-feeling medium and heavier weights, and it has a slightly firm hand that lends dramatic structure to a design. (Grace Kelly's wedding gown is one historical example.) It's a fabric of choice for special-occasion garments, and Mood customers have used it for everything from strapless mini-dresses to full-length ball gowns. *Peau de soie* (French for "skin of silk") is similar to duchesse satin, but is not as heavy and has a satin face on both sides (in other words, it's reversible).

(TIPS)

- Be forewarned, duchesse satin has a tendency to curl at the edges when cut. Hand-basting the seams (just outside the seam line, so the needle holes don't show) with silk thread will make the curl factor easier to deal as you machine-stitch.
- Always underline with silk organza when using duchesse satin. This way you can catch-stitch seam allowances and hems to the organza, so your stitches won't show on your garment.

> **"The effect I'm searching for is to have the fabric fall like liquid gold against the body."**
>
> —MARY MCFADDEN

Opposite:
1. Crepe-backed satin
2. Double-faced satin
3. Silk zibeline
4–5. Silk charmeuse
6. Duchesse satin
7. Double-faced satin
8. Silk zibeline

CHIFFON AND GEORGETTE

Sheer, sweet, and ethereal, chiffon conveys innocence and delicate beauty (that may be why it's a favorite of costume designers). Georgette is very close in appearance to chiffon but has a slightly denser crepe appearance—and is a bit easier to work with. Both make excellent fabrics to use as a top layer (overlay fabric) above an opaque layer, as sheer insets, and as ruffles, flowing scarves, or draped extensions. Synthetic forms of chiffon and georgette can look nearly as good as the silk versions, and beginning sewers may find them a little less challenging at the sewing machine.

(TIPS)

- Chiffon and georgette will get caught in your sewing machine's throat plate and bobbin area if you start sewing from the edge. Place a piece of pattern or tissue paper at the beginning of the seam and slightly overlapping the fabric, then sew from paper to fabric. Tear away the paper and tie the threads' ends together to secure the seam.

- Pinning and ripping out seams can damage and stress delicate fabrics like chiffon and georgette. Hand-baste seams and other parts of your garment instead of pinning; you'll find layers are less likely to shift while stitching.

- Because these fabrics' transparency reveals their seams, try French seams and very narrow, double-folded hems, so raw edges are enclosed and minimized. They take a little more time, but the end result is more professional and sophisticated looking.

TULLE

Pronounced "tool" and named after its French city of origin, tulle is a frothy, delicate netting found in ballerinas' tutus and brides' veils, as well as sheer overlays and crinolines. It is a type of mesh, but the fabric's structure is woven, rather than knit. **Silk tulle** is beautifully soft and fine, and ideal for layers and gathers in fine eveningwear. However, most commercial tulle is made of nylon, which is much tougher (and cheaper), and a better bet for anything that will not be visible on the outside of a garment (as well as little girls' tutus, which can take a beating during ballet class). Tulle, because of its airiness, is an effective way to create weightless volume; it offers a unique form of sheerness with varying depths of color if it's shirred or layered. **Novelty tulles** can come embroidered or flocked with dots, floral motifs, or lace patterns.

Point d'esprit is a variant of tulle with larger holes and dots of texture at the intersection of the yarns; it's often used in hatmaking.

(TIPS)

- Since tulle is mostly air, not fiber, you'll need to use stabilizing tape to secure seams.

- Hems can (and should) be left raw. Tulle doesn't unravel and would be difficult to hem anyway!

- Don't iron tulle, especially synthetic tulle, or it will disintegrate. If you must press, use a thick pressing cloth and low-heat iron.

- Use a roller foot or adhere a strip of tape along the bottom of the presser foot to alleviate snagging.

Opposite (top to bottom):
Pont d'esprit
Silk georgette
Silk tulle
Silk chiffon
Nylon tulle
Nylon tulle
Nylon tulle
Nylon tulle
Silk tulle
Silk tulle

Pressing sticks are magical tools that can be used in place of, or in addition to, an iron. In the case of delicate silks or anything with fusible interfacing, skip the iron and use the flat end of the stick along the split-open seam. Apply weight, and the stick will press open the seam without imprinting the seam allowance or the stitching marks, as an iron might.

> "I love the sculptural ability of silk gazar and how it gives me a chance to create new silhouettes. It's light but it has body."
>
> —STELLA NOLASCO

Above: A silk gazar gown from Angel Sanchez's spring/summer 2011 bridal collection. Gazar has a lot of body, which makes it ideal for sculptural silhouettes.

GAZAR

If you like fabrics that you can "sculpt," take a look at silk gazar. A favorite of drama-prone designers like Cristobal Balenciaga, Alber Elbaz at Lanvin, and Donna Karan, gazar is a plain, lightweight silk with a crisp hand that enables you to mold dramatic flounces, ruffles, and other architectural details. Often confused with heavier organzas, silk gazar has a slightly rougher hand; some gazars exhibit a gauzy or linen-ish appearance (the French word for gauze is *gaze*).

(TIPS)

- French seams and baby hems, in which raw edges are enclosed and minimized, look the best in gazar. They take a little more time, but the end result is a more professional and sophisticated-looking garment. Dramatically wide, double-fold hems also work as a design feature, especially at the bottom of a very full skirt.

- Keep garment details to a minimum and allow this fabric's sculptural qualities to dictate your design. Excessive seams and details will not only weigh silk gazar down, but you'll end up with a garment that's fussy, looks overworked, and has Tim Gunn telling you he's sorry, but it's time to clean up your work area.

Above (left to right):
Satin-backed silk organza
Silk gazar
Patterned silk organza
Silk gazar
Textured silk organza

ORGANZA

Organza is a sheer, nearly transparent, crisp silk with a split personality. On the one hand, it can be quite showy as a feature in special occasion garments, like a sheer blouse or elaborately ruffled dress. Several *Project Runway* designers have created new "fabrics" by placing colored organza atop a base fashion fabric, transforming the fashion fabric's look and feel. But organza is also a behind-the-scenes workhorse, serving both as an underlining staple and as the best press cloth around, due to its ability to withstand high heat and a transparency that allows you to see what you're pressing. Organza also comes in polyester and nylon varieties, but Mood clients find silk organza easier to work with and well worth the extra cost. One especially dramatic variety is satin organza, a heavier-weight silk organza with a satiny face on one side that looks stunning when shaped into curves and flounces.

(TIPS)

- Use heavy pattern weights to hold organza down while cutting; this fabric is super-shifty and floaty.
- If you're using organza for the body of a garment, sew French seams to present a neat appearance, because the seams will be visible.

Above: Crepe de chine

CREPE DE CHINE

Silk crepe de chine is one of Mood's greatest hits. Every designer loves and uses it. Lightweight with a plain weave and subtle texture, CDC (as it's known to industry insiders) has a matte finish or very subtle sheen and comes in three weights: two-ply, three-ply, and four-ply, with two-ply being the lightest (it's woven from two-ply yarns—that is, yarns that consist of two strands of silk fiber twisted together) and four-ply the heaviest and most luxurious. What is so appealing about silk crepe de chine is that it's elegant and tasteful without being flashy. A blouse sewn from silk crepe de chine looks expensive; a CDC jacket or coat lining looks like a high-end designer touch. Other applications include dresses, tops, wide-leg pants, and lingerie. It's also one of the only silks that can be machine-washed; try running thicker CDC through a machine with tennis balls before cutting and sewing for a more relaxed, sanded look and even more softness.

> **"If you're worried about silk's slipperiness, try silks that have some weight or friction, like crepes. They won't shift as much if they have friction or texture."**
>
> —VIKTOR LUNA, *PROJECT RUNWAY* SEASON 9

A professional-grade steamer is an investment worth making for any designer for a number of reasons; in the case of this technique, its steady blast of steam will do the job quickly. But if you don't have one, a travel steamer or steam iron held away from the fabric should do the trick. Lay the fabric flat on an ironing board or other steam-proof surface, and hold the steamer or iron ½" (12 mm) above the surface. Allow steam to seep into the fabric for a few seconds, and let the fabric dry before you move on to each new section. You can also fold the fabric and hang it over a hanger or rack to steam it; again, let the yardage dry completely before cutting. For a hands-off method, hang the fabric on a hanger over a bathtub of hot water. Leave it in the closed bathroom until the water cools and the fabric is fully dry.

HABUTAI (CHINA SILK)
(SEE PHOTO PAGE 124)

Habutai is the workhorse of the silk family, a plain weave that comes in a wide variety of colors and weights. While its popularity has waned some with the advent of better polyester fabrics on the market, it is one of the least expensive silks per yard. Many Mood customers and professional designers use lightweight habutai for lining their jackets and dresses, or sew blouses and tops from the heavier weights. Habutai can be machine-washed, and often softens up quite a bit once you do so, creating a more parachute-like feeling. Washing a habutai garment will also create wrinkled, puckered seams, but this can look cool with sporty topstitching.

(TIPS)

• If you're using habutai as a lining for a jacket, check first that it's opaque enough to conceal your jacket's seams and inner workings. Some habutais can be almost sheer.

• The lighter forms of habutai can be shifty like chiffons and georgettes. Add more control to your sewing by hand-basting or stitching seams with the fabric placed atop a 2"- (5-cm-) wide strip of parchment paper or pattern paper, then tear the paper away after sewing.

DUPIONI AND SHANTUNG
(SEE PHOTO PAGE 139)

"Slub" is the funny-sounding term for the raised bump that is created in a fabric when the yarn thickens or twists in the weaving. Sometimes slubs are flaws in a fabric and sometimes, as in the case of dupioni and shantung, they are a defining characteristic. Silk **dupioni** is a crisp fabric with a soft sheen that evokes both the 1960s glamour of Jacqueline Kennedy and sumptuous Indian saris. **Shantung** is the slightly lighter weight, less slubby version of dupioni. Both lend themselves perfectly to structured eveningwear, jackets, and coats, simple dresses and pants, tunics, and all sorts of home décor applications.

(TIPS)

• Dupioni and shantung fray like crazy. Some home sewers like to serge all their garment pieces' edges before sewing, just to prevent being overwhelmed by all of the silky threads.

• Silk dupioni and shantung seams are worthy of **Hong Kong seam finishes** (a term for covering the raw edges with bias binding), but if you don't have the time or inclination, then be sure to serge or pink the raw edges to prevent fraying.

• Warning: Hand- or machine-washing dupioni or shantung can cause their lovely sheen to disappear. Dry-clean only!

Opposite (top to bottom):
Silk dupioni with interfacing backing
Silk dupioni
Silk shantung
Silk taffeta
Silk taffeta
Silk faille
Silk bengaline (on roll)

FAILLE

First things first: In French, it's pronounced "fye," though an acceptable English pronunciation is "file." This elegant silk fabric evokes the ribs of a grosgrain ribbon with small cross-grain cords, a subtle sheen, and stiff drape. Designers often use faille for spring coats, jackets, and eveningwear, and it makes an excellent accent fabric on collars, pockets, and covered buttons. **Ottoman** and **bengaline** are similar to faille and can be equally elegant; both have slightly bigger ribs than faille, and ottoman's are the largest.

(TIPS)

- Match your garment to faille's drape. Architectural-type details, like a dramatic tuck or pleat, work well with a stiff fabric like faille, but it's far too substantial to form soft gathers.
- Steam-shrink any ottoman or bengaline with thicker ribs (cords) before you cut your fabric. Not only will this plump the cords and make them more pronounced, it will force the cotton inside the cords to shrink.
- Watch the placement of the horizontal ribs when cutting your garment pieces. They should be perpendicular to the pattern's grain line or cut on a consistent angle so that your garment has a balanced look.
- Minimize bulk at the seams by using organza, crepe de chine, or charmeuse as facing materials instead of the faille itself.
- Press seams open over a pressing stick to eliminate seam show-through, and never press too hard.

TAFFETA

Synonymous with party dresses, ball gowns, and that unmistakable swish-swish sound, taffeta is a lightweight fabric with a softly iridescent sheen and crisp hand that tends to crease and crumple. Like many fabrics that originated as silk, taffeta now comes in a variety of synthetic versions. Polyester and nylon taffetas are used for more technical garments, like anoraks, puffers, and windbreakers, plus sporting goods like sleeping bags and tents. Taffeta (the original silk variety) was even used to make the world's first hot air balloon in 1783!

(TIPS)

- Add body to your taffeta garment by underlining it in organza or tulle, or interlining with flannel.
- Press carefully—creases are very hard to remove!
- Keep garment designs on the simpler, more structural side to avoid lots of easing and pressing and fiddling, which could result in creases. Alternatively, take advantage of taffeta's natural body in extremely full, gathered, or pleated skirts and dresses.

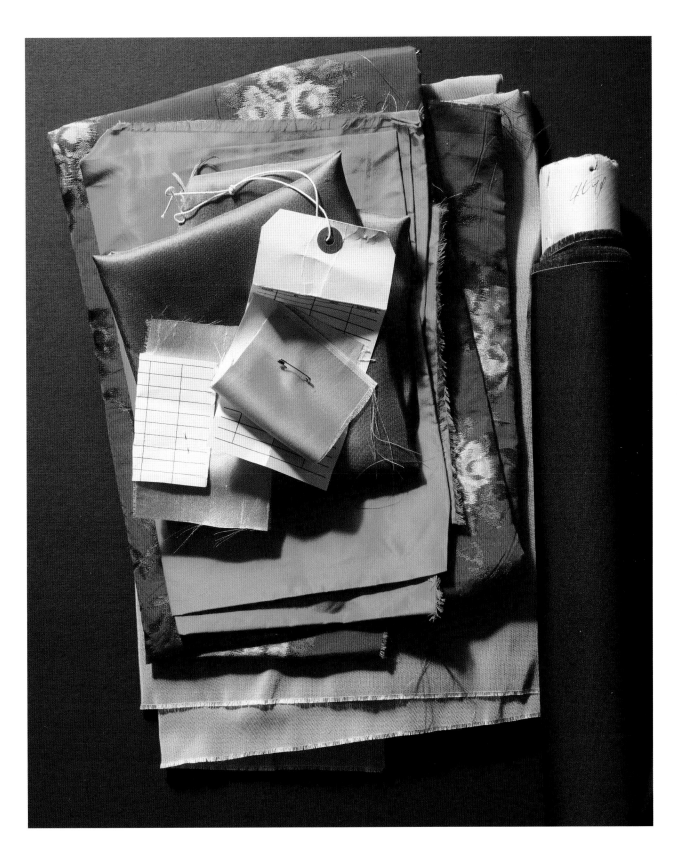

MIKADO SILK (SILK/WOOL BLEND)

Like duchesse satin but even more substantial due to its blended fiber content, mikado's somewhat stiff drape and exquisite folding capability work well for bold and structural pieces, like wedding dresses. The sheen of the fabric creates highs and lows that further accentuate the garment's drape and shape. You may also find silk taffeta-like fabric labeled "mikado."

(TIPS)

• Mikado silk is expensive. To be sure it works with your style, sew a test garment first from a stiff-ish fabric that mimics mikado silk's dramatic behavior. Look for a woven that doesn't collapse when you shape it into a cone.

• Silk/wool blends generally press well and can withstand higher heat, though always test on a scrap first.

SYNTHETIC SILKS

POLYESTER used to be a dirty word, but these days, some polyesters (most notably those from Japan) have all the beauty and fluidity of silk—and are much easier to care for (most are machine-washable). Some polys, as they're known informally, are afford-able alternatives to silk, while others are every bit as expensive! Handle silk-like polyester as you would the similar style of silk, but don't ever let a hot iron touch synthetic fiber, or it may melt. Use a press cloth and press from the wrong side of the fabric.

Opposite: An assortment of silk/poly blends
Above: Mikado Silk

BROCADE / JACQUARD

Brocade's name comes from the same root as broccoli: the Italian word for embossed cloth, *broccato*. Brocade isn't actually embossed, though; what distinguishes this class of fabrics is a secondary, non-structural weft pattern, which creates a raised appearance similar to embroidery. Though brocades can be made of silk, rayon, polyester, cotton, metallic synthetics, or some combination thereof, do not confuse the inexpensive synthetic brocades found in many fabric stores (often featuring a chinoiserie motif) with the sumptuous, high-quality brocades from designers like Carolina Herrera and Oscar de la Renta. Silk brocades are especially rich-looking, with striking floral, geometric, or animal patterns woven into color-intensive backgrounds, often with metallic highlights. Although it has a reputation as a more elegant, royal-feeling fabric for use in structured eveningwear, the new wave of brocades—as seen on the runways of Proenza Schouler and Narciso Rodriguez—feature modern motifs, and they're inventively draped or combined with not-so-fussy fabrics.

The term **jacquard** is sometimes used interchangeably with brocade. Jacquard, named after inventor Joseph Marie Jacquard, technically refers to the weaving technique and type of loom (a Jacquard loom) used to generate intricate weaves including brocade, damask, and matelassé. A **damask** fabric is produced using only one type of yarn instead of two or more, as in a brocade. Damask fabrics are thus more subtle than brocades, and are reversible; they are popular for use in interiors and are often made of fibers like linen, cotton, worsted wool, and synthetics. **Matelassé** fabrics, like brocades, feature a secondary weft; they are marked by a raised pattern that appears quilted or padded.

If your brocade has a large motif or print, take time to have a little strategy session about where you want the motifs to fall *before* you cut out your pattern. Stand in front of a mirror and drape the fabric on yourself, or drape it on your dress form. Avoid placing central motifs where you don't want to command attention; in other words, don't let a giant flower fall smack-dab on your derrière.

Opposite (top to bottom):
Silk tapestry
Silk matelassé
Silk jacquard/damask
Silk brocade
Silk matelassé

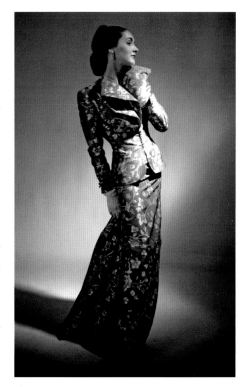

Above: A look from *Vogue*, October 1946. Brocade fabrics are a perennial favorite for elegant, high-end eveningwear.

//////////////////////////////////////

DENIS GRAMS

Manager, Silks,
Mood NYC

Hometown:
Johannesburg,
South Africa

Favorite fabric:
Brocades

//////////////////////////////////////

When the costume department of the *Star Wars* movies needs someone to hand-pick futuristic brocade fabrics to overnight to London, or the studio manager of a famous Seventh Avenue design house wants a suggestion for a grouping of fabrics to use in a collection, or a pop star comes in and wants a tour, whom do they call? Denis, Mood's resident fine-fabrics guru. A soft-spoken man with a distinctive braided ponytail, Denis is arguably the busiest salesperson on Mood's floor (and that's saying a lot), tending to VIPs and using his sixth sense for color and texture to create many of the fabric and color boards peppered throughout the store. He's a swatch wizard,

able to combine fabrics in unexpected ways; top designers count on him to swatch for them when they can't come to Mood themselves.

Denis came to the United States to attend the University of Michigan, where he studied political science before making his way to New York. A recreational sewer, he fell into assisting, and then managing production and sample studios for a series of Garment District fashion houses, including Marc Jacobs and the eveningwear designer Pamela Dennis. So popular is Denis among Broadway costumers that the outfits for a character in *A Midsummer Night's Dream*, Starveling the tailor, were even inspired by him!

(TIPS)

• Brocades tend to fray. Serge any raw edges that may be handled a lot before it's time to sew that section.

• If you're using a metallic brocade, especially a polyester metallic, test-press first on a scrap with your iron's heat on low and use a press cloth. Metallics tend to scorch and melt.

Opposite: Silk velvets
(left to right):

Solid silk velvet
Panné silk velvet
Burnout/dévoré silk velvet
Crushed silk velvet
Burnout/dévoré silk velvet
Panné silk velvet

VELVET

Plush and sumptuous, **velvet** has been the fabric of nobility since ancient times. King Richard II of England refused to wear anything else. In the comedy classic *Coming to America* (1988), a heavily disguised Eddie Murphy famously asks James Earl Jones, playing a king, of his lion pelt: "This is beautiful. What is it, velvet?" Velvet is distinguished by a dense raised pile and decadent drape. It can be made from silk, rayon, cotton, polyester, or acetate, though the silk and rayon varieties are the most luxurious.

Smooth, even styles of velvet are just the tip of the iceberg. **Burnout** or **dévoré** (French for "devoured") velvets are made of a blend of viscose pile on a silk backing; a chemical solution dissolves the viscose, etching semi-transparent patterns into the fabric. (You'll see this technique used sometimes in rayon-blend T-shirts, too.) **Crushed velvet**, a quintessential '90s look, has a mashed pile, creating a play of light and shadow; **panné velvet** is pressed in one continuous direction to produce a dazzling sheen. Velvet used to be considered a special-occasion fabric, but it can work equally well as a luxe option for daytime wear. (In case you're wondering, **velveteen** is usually made of cotton, and is both stiffer and duller than velvet; **velour** is the knitted variation of velvet.

Because of its pile and its tendency to show every mistake, most home sewers and fashion students have velvet on their list of most-feared fabrics. (Even Tim Gunn has warned *Project Runway* contestants away

ELIZABETH SOLES

Sales Associate,
Silks Department,
Mood NYC

Hometown:
Detroit, Michigan

Favorite fabric:
Printed crepe de chine. "People see silk and they're afraid of it because they think that it's going to be difficult to work with, but crepe de chine is so easy. It's like working with cotton."

Elizabeth's love for fashion started early. "I've been making things for myself since I was a kid," she recalls. Fashion, she believes, is at the apex between art and function. She lights up when working with customers, eager to help them find the right type of silk for their creation.

After going to school for fashion design in Chicago, Elizabeth moved to New York City in 2012 to immerse herself in the design field. A job at Mood, she thought, would be a crash course. "I figured I would learn a lot about fabric. I would meet a lot of people. And I really have."

Elizabeth loves working with silk— "It's luxurious and it's nice to be able to touch something so pretty every day. It's always inspiring when you're working with the raw material and seeing what people are doing with it." And the opportunity to drape mannequins at the store provides her with even more inspiration. "I get to see how the fabric moves," Elizabeth says. "This hands-on experience teaches me about pretty much every aspect of it."

from velvet unless they already have experience sewing it.) Choose a garment design that's very simple with few seams and details, and cut your pattern pieces with the nap facing the same way, and that's half the battle.

(TIPS)

- For your first velvet garment, try something basic, like a pullover top or tunic with dropped shoulders and a loose fit. Sew a muslin if the pattern needs to be fitted first, and check the nap twice before you cut; ripping out seams from velvet is a no-no.

- Decide which way you want the nap to fall by draping the velvet on your body before cutting. While it may feel smoother to the touch to have the nap facing downward, fabrics with piles often look richer with the nap facing upward.

- A walking foot can help keep the velvet from wiggling around while you stitch. When sewn with right (pile) sides together, velvet tends to shift out of position. Hand-basting seams can help control the fabric layers, too.

- Exercise extreme caution while pressing so you don't flatten the pile. A needleboard is a special tool for pressing velvet; if you're crazy for velvet, consider investing in one, use a thick towel otherwise. Press the velvet pile down, with the lightest possible touch. You can use a scrap of velvet as a press cloth.

Above:
1. Dark pink silk noil
2. Light pink silk moiré
3. Purple silk noil (folded)
4. Cranberry-print silk foulard
5. Purple raw silk

OTHER SILK VARIETIES

A few additional terms you might encounter when shopping for silks:

Moiré is an effect found in silks that creates a wavy appearance, sometimes like wood.

Foulard refers to a twill-weave silk designed for ties or scarves with a multi-colored printed pattern. The French word for "scarf," foulard can also refer to a scarf or ascot itself. Tie silks don't have to be used for ties; they can make fanciful linings or contrast binding, or be used for a garment itself.

Noil is made from the short fibers left over at the end of the combing and carding process in sericulture. It has an earthy, slightly nubby texture that might be mistaken for a raw cotton. However, it has a soft, cozy feel and drape that makes it an appealing (and more expensive) alternative.

Raw silk is silk that hasn't been cleaned or degummed; it has a rough, stiff texture almost like burlap. You won't find this at Mood, and if you do find it, it's likely to have a distinct smell from the silk gum residue. It's hard to remove without actually boiling the fabric or washing it in a hot, soapy solution—which is why most fabric stores stick to silk that's already been finished by mills or converters.

Other Fabrics

OME FABRICS FALL OUTSIDE of Mood's main categories, but are every bit as appealing— and as important to know about—as cotton, wool, silk, and knits. This chapter organizes these outliers into three general groups:

Novelty fabrics really run the gamut, but all can produce spectacular design effects. From elaborate beading to romantic lace, these unique fabrics can't be categorized by fiber content or structure. The main attraction— and the common thread, so to speak—is their specific type of texture or embellishment.

Leather, fur, and skins are animal hides used to make clothing or accessories. These are the only types of fabric not sold by the yard; instead, they're sold by the skin, hide, or pelt. For simplicity's sake, faux leathers and furs will be included in this section of the chapter, though they technically fall under the next category, nonwovens.

Nonwovens are, like their name suggests, not woven (or knitted) at all; they're created by machine-forming a sheet of material directly from fiber or liquid (as in vinyl and felt). Fleece, felt, films, and some types of interfacing fall into this category, as do the synthetic versions of leather and fur.

Because every fabric in this chapter is a bit different, instructions for care and sewing tips are addressed individually for each fabric type.

NOVELTY FABRICS

Fabrics whose key feature is their surface treatment—whether it's embellishment, coating, or lawmination—are listed alphabetically here.

BEADS, SEQUINS, AND PAILLETTES
(SEE PHOTO PAGE 148)

For pure design razzle-dazzle, nothing beats fabric adorned with delicate beads or shimmering discs. Sequins are small and usually attached through a hole in the center to sit flush against the fabric; paillettes (pronounced "pie-ettes") are usually much larger, and dangle downward from a hole that's close to the edge (the resulting effect is reminiscent of fish scales). These fabrics make terrific tops and dramatic dresses; they can also be used as contrast or trim elements (like a pocket or sleeves) or even for more casual looks like T-shirts or sweatshirts. These days, sequins, beads, and paillettes can even have a more muted, less shiny look, or be made of soft materials like leather. The only downside is that they're difficult to handle and sew. Running hard beads or discs through your machine is a guaranteed way to break a needle (if not the machine itself). Read on for tips on how to keep your machine, your garment, and your sanity intact.

(TIPS)

• Dry-clean only. Leave these delicate creations to the professionals!

- Store and handle with care to avoid creasing the base fabric or its embellishments. Hang the fabric or carefully fold it; don't let it crumple up in a ball, and don't put things on top of it.
- Be prepared: These fabrics take longer to cut and sew than others. Plan your schedule accordingly, and don't rush.
- Stick to simpler styles, like shift dresses, shell tops, or straight skirts—the fewer seams, the better.
- Many embellished fabrics are directional, so cut your patterns using a with-nap layout.
- Don't let an iron touch the surface—especially in the case of sequins or paillettes, they'll probably melt.

> "For me, it's important to anticipate where fashion is heading."
>
> —MIUCCIA PRADA

- Use a thread to mark the stitching line of each cut pattern piece, and remove sequins or beads that will get in the needle's way. You can reattach them later to cover up bald spots along the seam (or just cover up the seam, period). In the case of small beads, you can also smash them with a hammer to clear them out of the way; sequins can be clipped carefully off their securing stitches. Avoid cutting the threads that hold the embellishments in place, as this can cause an entire row or patch of beads or sequins to fall off.
- Don't use fusible interfacing with these fabrics; stick to sew-ins. Cut facings from a coordinating, non-embellished fabric for more comfort during wear.
- Use a longer stitch length, like 3.5 mm. Alternatively, consider hand-sewing the seams. It takes a little longer, but you'll save time by not having to remove the embellishment from the seam allowances.
- Raw edges are difficult to finish. Consider lining your garment.
- Cover the floor near your sewing area for easier cleanup; the floor will likely be covered with beads or sequins by the time you're done.

Above: Paillettes create a fish-scale effect and come in many shapes and sizes; they can even be translucent, as seen on Prada's fall/winter 2011 runway.

BONDED FABRICS

Bonded fabrics are made by fusing two or more layers of fabric together with heat or glue. Often, but not always, one fabric is a knit or woven and the other is a nonwoven—that is, a layer of vinyl, film, fleece, or foam. You might find wool bonded to polyester, or cotton bonded to a novelty vinyl, or leather bonded to a stretch synthetic (**stretch leather**—see page 164). They usually have beautiful, crisp body and are often, because of their layered structure, very warm. They're also usually double-faced, which opens up all sorts of design possibilities. Use them in tailored styles with strong silhouettes, like coats, jackets, skirts, and dresses. Tougher bonded fabrics can also be used for bags.

Neoprene is a classic example of a bonded fabric. It's made from fused-together layers of foam and fabric, usually a synthetic knit jersey. Though it's commonly used in surf and scuba gear—which is why it's also become popular as a swimwear fabric—neoprene has great body and strength and a cool, futuristic feel, which is why it has become increasingly popular for dramatically structured coats, jackets, skirts, and dresses, and even T-shirts and bags. Just remember, there's a reason it's used for wetsuits: it's very warm!

Note that neoprene—especially thicker versions—can be tough for a home sewing machine to handle. If your machine can't manage two layers of it, consider sewing abutted seams: Place garment sections side by side with cut edges touching, and join them with a wide zigzag stitch. Alternatively,

a high-quality fabric glue does a good job of bonding lapped seams.

(TIPS)

- The layers of bonded fabric can be separated in high heat, which can break down glues. Take care not to iron or wash the fabric in hot water. Hand-wash cold, and don't tumble-dry with heat. When in doubt, ask a sales associate whether dry cleaning is appropriate.
- Bonded fabrics can be bulky. Use a walking foot for ease of sewing.
- Bonded fabrics usually—but not always—are fray-free and can be left raw-edged. Bulkier versions might be better off with seam allowances serged or enclosed with bias tape, rather than pressed open.
- Be sure to use the appropriate needle size for the thickness of your fabric. Discuss with a salesperson if you aren't sure.

COATED FABRICS

When a surface treatment is applied to a fabric—often to keep water out, but sometimes for decorative purposes as well—the fabric has been coated. These fabrics are almost always used for outerwear, such as raincoats, but some designers like their crisper hand and technical look and feel for other garments, like dresses or skirts. Coating often changes the hand and drape of a fabric quite dramatically. **Waxed cotton** is a traditional coated fabric in which woven cotton is coated with wax to keep out water; these days, manufacturers apply micro wax and other synthetic and technical waxes. Its

Opposite:
1. Waxed cotton
2–3. Plastic-coated rainwear
4. Stretch leather
5. Neoprene

152/ THE MOOD GUIDE TO FABRIC AND FASHION

classic design examples are the traditional British hunting and racing jackets from Barbour and Belstaff. Waxed cotton can show creases and wear quite easily, but that's what gives it a distinctive look as it wears in. Fabrics can also be coated with liquid rubber, spray foam, or just about anything. They're also generally strong enough to be used for accessories, like bags.

(TIPS)

- Wash in cold water, and keep the coating away from heat, or it might melt.

- Avoid storing coated fabrics with too many folds and creases, because they could be permanent. Hang the fabric, or roll it onto a fabric roll.

- Ripping out stitches is not an option with coated fabrics; needle holes are permanent. Mood never recommends pinning into the body of fabric, but it's an especially important rule to keep in mind here.

- Before pressing, test the iron's heat on a scrap of fabric. Use a press cloth and low heat, and don't press on the coated side. If the coating melts under even the lowest heat, use a roller or other tool to flatten seams with pressure alone.

- The coated side isn't designed to come into contact with skin; it might feel rough or rubbery, and it's not breathable. Keep the right side out in your design.

- Coated fabrics tend not to ravel, so seams can be pinked, and raw hems can even be a design detail in some cases.

> **"If you really know the [fashion] business, you know how much money it really takes to use special duchess satin or lace— $40 million a collection."**
>
> —VERA WANG

LACE

Dainty, delicate lace—an openwork fabric distinguished by ornamental patterns formed either with no background fabric, or on a ground of net or mesh—might be the most romantic fabric on the planet. It arose in its modern form in Europe in the 15th or 16th century, when it was handmade for nobility and the upper classes. Today, most laces are made by machine. They can be embroidered on mesh, tulle, or another netting base fabric, or created by the knotting, twisting, or crocheting of separate threads. They can be made of cotton, silk, metallic threads, or synthetics; be used as trim or the body of a garment; or even be stretchy. Lace is commonly used for evening dresses and lingerie, but can also be used in smaller doses as a decorative element on daywear, whether as trim, edging, or a transparent layer over a different fabric. It pairs beautifully with silk and velvet.

Lace comes in a few different formats for different purposes. **Edging lace** has one straight edge (the heading) and one scalloped edge, which forms hems on a garment. **Insertion lace** has a straight edge on both sides and can be sewn into pattern pieces with seams; it's symmetrical, in other words. **Tape lace** comes in strips to be used as edging or trim.

These are some types of lace you are likely to find at Mood and other fabric stores:

Needle lace (sometimes called needlepoint lace) is embroidered with a single needle; it is basically made with a variant of the buttonhole stitch, but crafted into patterns that

Above:
1. Chantilly lace
2. Crocheted lace
3. Embroidered bridal lace
4. Guipure lace
5–6. Broderie Anglaise (eyelet)
7. Embroidered lace
8. Bridal lace

are sometimes fantastically elaborate. Needle lace has either no ground fabric, or a very lightweight, sheer mesh ground. Some noteworthy styles include **Alençon lace**, **Battenberg lace**, and **filet lace**.

Broderie anglaise is actually a large-scale type of cutwork embroidery (sections cut out between embroidery patterns). Unlike other laces, broderie anglaise has solid fabric ground supporting it. Named for its popularity in England (it actually originated in eastern Europe), broderie anglaise is usually made from a finely woven cotton base and looks almost like lace that has been enlarged—that is, the scale is much larger, making the fabric sturdier than most lace. A less-complex version of this is what we commonly refer to as **eyelet lace**.

Bobbin lace is made from multiple threads woven together to create patterns. **Chantilly lace**, named for its French city of origin, is one famous example; it's characterized by a very fine net ground. Another is **guipure lace,** which is generally quite thick and lacks a net background.

Crocheted lace is just as it sounds: crocheted; it's generally made to imitate needle lace styles from Venice and Spain.

Bridal lace, as a category, covers many types of lace; it generally refers to fine laces that are usually white.

Mass-market lace is far less expensive than the delicate, traditional, usually European-made laces used for bridal gowns and high-end eveningwear. It's typically flatter in texture than fine lace, and often made from polyester or a blend. **Stretch lace** can be used as a body fabric, not just a trim, for intimates as well as dresses, skirts, and tops. **Raschel lace** is a less delicate knitted fabric with a lace-like openwork pattern.

(TIPS)

• Handle with care and keep sharp objects away. Lace can snag easily.

• Fine lace should be dry-cleaned only once it's been made into a garment. In some cases, you can hand-wash it gently before cutting and sewing.

• Mass-market lace, like stretch lace, can in many cases be hand-washed or machine-washed on a gentle cycle, but do not put it in a heat dryer.

• Many types of lace don't have a "grain," so you can position pattern pieces in any direction; this means you can place the motifs to highlight the lines of the garment.

• Lace—especially fine lace—is very delicate. If you're a beginner, consider sending your sewing project to a professional tailor.

• Use a press cloth, and test heat settings on scraps. Polyester and nylon lace can melt with the heat of an iron!

• Use a finer universal needle—try a size 60/8.

• Be sure to match lace motifs at seamlines when possible. This will, in many cases, increase the required amount of yardage. Alternatively, you can appliqué separate motifs from scrap lace to conceal areas where a perfect match is impossible.

• Use a zigzag stitch when sewing lace to a non-lace fabric, and to sew lapped seams and appliqués.

• When sewing lace to lace, be careful not to let the fabric get sucked into your feed dogs. Place a strip of paper under the seam as you sew to stabilize the delicate fabric, and tear the paper away gently after sewing.

• Lace generally doesn't ravel; you can cut around the motifs' edges to form the hems of a garment, or cut out separate motifs for appliqués.

Below: Lace trims
1. Lace edging
2. Beaded lace
3. Filet lace
4. Lace edging
5. Alençon lace
6. Battenberg lace tape
7. Bobbin lace
8. Insertion lace
9. Filet lace

Above: An assortment of metallics

1. Metallic finish
2. Metallic fibers in a bouclé
3. Metallic finish
4. Lamé
5. Metal fibers

METALLIC FABRICS

Some fabrics have actual **metal fibers** woven into them; this allows them to literally be bent, molded, and crumpled, after which they'll hold their shape. Metal can be blended with silk, linen, wool—just about anything—to create either a crinkled or voluminous shape.

Some fibers have a metallic finish but are not literally made of metal. **Lamé**, which is a woven or knit fabric made fully or in part with metallic yarns, is not generally made with actual metal but with metallic-coated synthetic material such as polyester or plastic. It can be gold or silver in tone, colorful, or even holographic. It has a glam, disco-fied appeal and a liquid-like sheen that makes it ideal for draped styles and evening dresses.

(TIPS)

- With fabrics that include real metal, the fibers should be fine enough and the percentage in the fabric blend should be small enough that it won't mess up your machine. Test tension and needle type and size on a scrap before sewing.
- Anchor pattern pieces with weights rather than pins, and avoid pinning in the body of the garment. Metallic fibers are delicate and easily snagged or broken.
- Use sharp scissors to ensure clean cuts.
- Lamé tends to ravel easily; metallic fiber can scratch the skin, especially on raw edges. Enclose seam edges with bias tape.

PLEATED FABRICS

While pleating can be achieved at home with a steam iron and a ruler or pleating board, some fabrics come pre-pleated, or have been pleated post-production by designers, who send them to be pleated with heat or chemicals. Silk, cotton, polyester, and even leather can be pleated, though if you plan to pleat fabric at home by folding and pressing it, the fabric should contain some synthetic fiber in order to retain the pleats for longer. Pleating has a dramatic look and creates beautiful volume and movement. In addition to garments (usually skirts), it can also be used for trim elements, inserts, sleeves, or overlays. Narrow accordion and sunburst pleats (these radiate from a central point outward, and are wider at the bottom than at the top), as well as Fortuny-style, super-narrow pleats are among the most common pleats you'll find. You can also send your own fabric to a commercial pleater and have it pleated to order. Bear in mind the fabric must have some synthetic fiber content for the pleats to be permanent.

(TIPS)

- Pressing can sometimes iron out the pleats (in the case of micro-pleats or other small textural pleats). Avoid using an iron directly on the fabric.
- Synthetic fabrics that have been pleated can often be washed in cool water, by hand or in the machine on a gentle cycle. Lay the garment flat or hang it to dry.
- Plan your pattern layout carefully when using pleated fabrics. For the best drape, place vertical seams along a pleat.

Opposite: An assortment of pleated fabrics (top to bottom):

Pleated cotton blend
Super-narrow pleats, poly blend
Super-narrow pleats, poly blend
Fortuny-style silk blend
Pleated leather
Fortuny-style silk blend
Pleated chiffon/poly blend

"[Fortuny] has some secret way of pleating, so that his gowns cling to you alluringly forever and ever, and you can roll them up and tuck them into the corner of your suitcase without a thought about wrinkles."

—*VOGUE*, 1934

- Try narrow corded piping as an edge finish at necklines and armholes; a narrow hem, simple zigzag, or overlock stitch is often sufficient as a hem on fabrics with very narrow pleats.
- Pleats won't survive washing in cotton, rayon, or linen garments—they'll have to be re-pressed from scratch after each laundering. To make pressing easier on wider knife, box, or inverted pleats, edgestitch some or all of the folds (if you don't want the edgestitching to show, stitch only the underlying folds). This creates a permanent guideline for re-pressing the pleats.

Whether to choose real or faux fur or leather depends on a variety of factors—your ethical stance, your budget, and the look and feel you're after. Real fur and leather have an authentic, luxurious hand; however, because they come in skins or pelts rather than by the yard, they can be tricky to cut and match. No two are alike, and imperfections are the norm, so take extra care when planning your cutting. Faux varieties have come a long way; they're easier to cut and sew, and come in novelty colors and textures that can be even better than the real thing.

FUR AND FAUX FUR

Though perennially controversial because of animal-welfare concerns, **fur** is still popular for its unparalleled warmth and softness. Mood, as a supplier of fashion fabrics, remains neutral in this debate; the New York store carries some varieties of real fur to meet demand, including mink, fox, and goat. However, the quality and breadth of **faux furs**—made from polyester, acrylic, nylon, or other manufactured fibers—on the market today is dazzling. Some are so lifelike, it's hard to tell the difference. In other cases, faux fur isn't meant to look like real fur at all; novelty textures and colors create distinctive furry looks far more fantastical than anything found in nature. Faux fur is also inexpensive compared to real fur, lacks imperfections, and comes in yardage rather than pelts. Fur, either real or faux, can be used not only for outerwear, but also to make garments, or as trim on collars, cuffs, or even bags. If you choose to work with it, consider repurposing scraps (or even old jackets and

Above: Not just for coats: A dress with fur trim from J Mendel's fall/winter 2013 ready-to-wear collection.

Above: An assortment of real pelts/skins; long- and short-haired furs.

coats) to make smaller items so that the excess material doesn't go to waste.

Shearling is a type of fur made from sheepskin with its fur evenly shorn. Soft and warm, the napped side is often used on the inside of garments for winter warmth and comfort, though it can also be reversed for a furry look. **Faux shearling** often has synthetic suede on one side and fleece on the other.

Ponyskin is a flat-surfaced, durable, hairy type of fur that's actually more often made from cow hides than horse hides. It's popular for shoes, belts, and bags as well as jackets or elements of trim, such as pockets. Faux versions are also available.

Long-haired fur and faux fur have especially deep, shaggy piles that create dramatic volume in overall garments and interesting detail in trim. Long-haired naps will move very clearly in one direction, and must be matched among pattern pieces.

(TIPS)

• Store fur on a flat surface.

• Real fur should be professionally cleaned only. Faux fur can sometimes be hand- or machine-washed, most often with shorter-pile varieties. Ask your fabric salesperson. Never tumble-dry faux fur with heat.

• Keep irons away, especially from faux fur, which will melt in an instant.

• Designers who work with real fur use special machines that only professional tailors have on hand. Real fur is also very expensive, which is why it might be worth handing off to a pro if you're inexperienced.

//

DMITRY BYALIK

Manager, Leather
and Fur, Mood NYC

Hometown:
Brooklyn by way
of Ukraine

Favorite fabric:
Black leather of any
variety. "I just love a
dark aesthetic."

//

Dmitry arrived in New York from Ukraine with his family as an 11-year-old, and soon found himself drawn to the fashion world—especially, he says, the goth-romantic aesthetic of designer Rick Owens. He went on to attend the Art Institute of New York, interning with John Varvatos, Ralph Rucci, and Asher Levine. "But I didn't really want to work for another designer," Dmitry says. "Mood allows me to do my own thing."

The one-of-a-kind bags Dmitry creates in his free time (check them out at dmitrybyaliknyc.com) are certainly his own thing: They straddle the line between fashion and fine art. He molds leather to the shapes of skulls, guns, and other macabre instruments, transforming them into functional three-dimensional sculptures. (He also uses the same technique in his fine-art practice, which consists mostly of leather wall installations.) Most of his commissions, he says, come from the U.K., where punk was born and continues to thrive. And how, he is asked, does he get his leathers to stay permanently in such elaborate shapes? "That's my secret," he says, laughing.

- The thicker and deeper the fur, the trickier it is to work with. Choose low-pile varieties like ponyskin or shearling for the easiest at-home experience.
- All fur has a nap. Cut all pattern pieces facing the same way, and take care to avoid inconsistent markings or discolored areas when using the real thing.
- Cut fur (real or fake) with the wrong side up. Use sharp scissors or a razor blade to cut only the skin or backing, taking care not to cut the hairs of the fur. Then gently pull the hairs apart. This prevents a big, hairy mess in your sewing area, and will look polished along the seams. You can brush hairs back into place after sewing.
- To reduce bulk along seamlines, you can shave the seam allowances, using a small, electric hair clipper. Do this before or after the seam is sewn, but be careful not to clip the stitching.
- Comb hairs along the cut edges toward the center to prevent them from getting caught in the sewing machine.
- Hand-baste cut pieces together before sewing. This is worth the investment in time, as fur can misbehave in the machine.
- Use a longer stitch length (2.5 to 3 mm) and a narrow zigzag stitch.
- Consider using a walking foot to keep the top layer of fur running smoothly through the machine.
- Test scraps with denim-weight and leather needles.
- Vacuum stray hairs from your sewing machine, including the bobbin area, regularly during construction.
- After sewing the seam, use a rat-tail comb to pull all the pile to the right side of the fabric, and to comb it over the seamline.
- Use a tape lint roller for quick cleanup of your sewing area. Remove hair or lint from your sewing machine after each project.

Opposite: Faux furs
(top to bottom):

Long-pile faux fur
Surface-dyed short-pile
  faux fur
Faux mink
Faux lambskin

Above: An assortment of
real leather and suede.

LEATHER AND SUEDE

Rich, supple, and luxurious, leather is
beloved for its durability, comfort, versatile
look, and the way it softens over time. It
comes in a variety of weights and thicknesses
and can be used for anything from tough-as-
nails motorcycle jackets to delicate dresses.

The thickest varieties are **hides**, which
come from larger animals like cows and buf-
falo; these are so durable that they can even
be used as rugs.

Lambskin is the lightest and softest leather;
Dmitry recommends this for home sewers.

Perforated leather has small holes in
it for increased breathability and flexibil-
ity. It's great for garments, like simple tops
or dresses.

Reptile skins such as snakeskin are on the
small side, and thus more appropriate for
accessories or trim, rather than for garments.

Goatskin is easy to sew, but tends to stretch;
for this reason, it's best used for styles that
don't have a tight fit.

Washed leather has a drapey quality, and
can be used for softer silhouettes like skirts
and dresses. It may be machine-washable;
ask your fabric salesperson to be sure.

Stretch leather has been fused to stretch
fibers so that it can stretch and recover on the
body. It's a brilliant choice for pants, leggings,
and fitted dresses and skirts.

Patent leather is coated with a high-gloss
finish. It has a stiff, sturdy hand, which
makes it best suited for accessories. In some
cases, it can be used for very stiff, structured

garments, but it tends to crack and crease when bent.

Suede is leather with a brushed, napped surface. Because it has a nap, take care to match direction and surface appearance when cutting pieces.

(TIPS)

- While a few leathers are machine-washable, the cleaning of most is best left to professionals.
- Store leathers laid out flat or gently rolled around a tube. If they're left in creased and crinkled position over time, they may permanently stretch or wrinkle.
- Unlike fabric, leather comes in the form of skins rather than yardage, so the layout of each pattern will vary depending on the size and consistency of the skin. Fortunately, you can look at the entire skin and even bring your pattern to see how many skins you'll need. Be sure to cut around imperfections and keep an eye out for variations in color and consistency, and match along the seamlines of adjacent garment pieces.
- Thicker leathers aren't made for home sewing machines. Use a professional leather tailor, or hand-sew. For a home sewing machine, try lambskin, stretch leather, washed leather, or other thin leathers.
- Use a wedge-point needle designed for leather (these may be labeled "Leather needles") in a heavier gauge, such as 90/14 or 100/16.
- Leather tends to stick as it passes under the presser foot. A Teflon presser foot will

solve the problem, as will sticking a piece of Scotch tape to the bottom of the foot.
- Use 100% polyester thread; the tannins in some skins and hides can cause cotton thread to deteriorate.
- Set your sewing machine for a stitch length of 2.5 mm for lightweight, thin leather, and longer for thicker skins.
- Leather doesn't fray, so its seams require no finishing. Raw hems are also possible.
- Many types of seams are possible with leather, including lapped seams.
- To press open seams, apply leather adhesive or rubber cement between the seam allowances and the wrong side of the fabric and use a wallpaper roller to flatten them.
- Practice with scraps on your machine before sewing pattern pieces. Removing stitches from leather will leave permanent holes.

> "My job is to create beautiful, luxurious things. I love that people come into the store and don't even know that something is organic or in faux leather. That's the biggest challenge, having people not notice."
>
> —STELLA MCCARTNEY

Below: Faux leather and suede (top to bottom):

Faux cow hide
Faux suede
Embossed (with dots) faux suede
Faux ostrich skin

FAUX LEATHER AND SUEDE

Faux leathers and suedes look and feel better than ever these days. They're affordable, durable, can often be machine-washed, have perfectly even consistency, and are sold by the yard rather than the skin. Plus, they're quite easy to cut and work with, as long as you use the right needle. Some of these fabrics are backed with a layer of polyester or cotton knit or woven fabric for better breathability against the skin.

(TIPS)

- Because faux leather and suede are synthetic, they'll melt upon contact with heat. Use weights or wallpaper rollers to press.

- Use wedge-shaped needles as you would with regular leather; if those aren't available, use a heavier needle (from 10 to 16, depending on the fabric's thickness). Some faux suede behaves like a tight knit, and works best with a stretch needle.

- Faux suede may be easier for laying out pattern pieces than the real thing, but it still has a nap. Be sure to arrange pattern pieces accordingly.

- Like real leather and suede, faux varieties retain holes even after stitches are removed. Don't pin body pieces together, and try not to make sewing mistakes!

NONWOVENS

From felt to fusible interfacing, nonwovens may not be the first thing you think of when you think of fabric—but this is an important category, both for fashion and function. Fabrics in this section are listed alphabetically.

Above (top to bottom):
Wool felt
Acrylic felt
Wool felt
Polyester felt
Fur felt

FELT

Formed from wool, fur, rayon, polyester, or fibrous industrial refuse, felt is created by the high-pressure mashing of fibers into a flat sheet. It may resemble woven wool, and be equally easy to work with, but on a structural level it's different. Felt tends to have a stiffer hand and great body, which is why it's favored for structured, tailored styles (and, as the team at Mood has noticed, big, dramatic Halloween costumes). Novelty felts can be veritable works of art, with beautiful variations in color and texture. Because it's neither knit nor woven, felt can be left raw at its edges and sewn with lapped seams—and it often is, for a more organic look. (You can create your own felted fabrics by machine-washing certain sweater knits, wool jersey, and woven wools. This creates a dense fabric with a similar look and feel to felt.)

(TIPS)

- Seek out real wool felt for fine garments, such as coats. Save the cheap synthetic felt for arts and crafts projects (or Halloween), and don't let it touch your skin—synthetic felt can be irritating.

- Use a medium-sized universal needle.

- Test stitch lengths and tension on your machine before sewing pattern pieces. The thicker the felt, the longer the stitch length.

- Use sharp scissors or blades to cut felt. It tends to be very thick, and can pull and weaken at the hands of a dull blade.

- Felt's fuzzy surface can get stuck in feed dogs. Try sandwiching felt between sheets of tissue paper to smooth it through your machine. With a small hand vacuum, clean lint from the bobbin area frequently.

- Lapped seams work well with felt to reduce bulk.

- Felt doesn't ravel, so you can leave it with raw hems—these can even be a design detail.

FILMS

Nonwovens made from sheets of liquid that have been solidified are **films**. Usually, because they're non-porous, they are bonded or coated onto other, more skin-friendly fabrics. However, you might find **vinyl, plastic, polyurethane, PVC, latex**, or **rubber** on their own. Vinyl (the term Mood uses for the category, which can also cover plastic, polyurethane or polyvinyl chloride [PVC]) can be used for outerwear, bags, or structured, shiny separates. It can also form a top layer outside of another fabric.

As for latex and rubber, these stretchy, tacky materials are more likely to be used for catsuit costumes than for everyday clothing, but adventurous designers have been known to experiment with them. However, unless you're feeling avant-garde (think of Catwoman, or Marnie's infamous plastic dress in *Girls*), stick to bonded or coated versions that have another textile layered beneath.

(TIPS)

- Films don't allow moisture from the skin to evaporate. Avoid having them sit next to skin, or you'll get hot (even Marnie on *Girls* eventually removed her dress before the night was over).
- Depending on the thickness of the fabric, you can use a universal, sharp, or leather needle. Set the machine for a stitch length of at least 3 mm, to avoid perforating the seamlines too much.
- Keep heat far, far away from these easily melted fabrics. Use a wallpaper roller to press seams.
- Seams and hems can be kept raw; you might also use binding for a decorative look in the case of transparent films.
- Keep seams and design details to a minimum. The fabric is the statement.
- In the case of stretchy films like rubber and latex, use a stretch stitch.

Opposite:
1. Polyvinyl chloride (PVC)
2. Metallic-coated vinyl
3. Polyurethane
4. Clear plastic
5. Latex/rubber
6. Vinyl

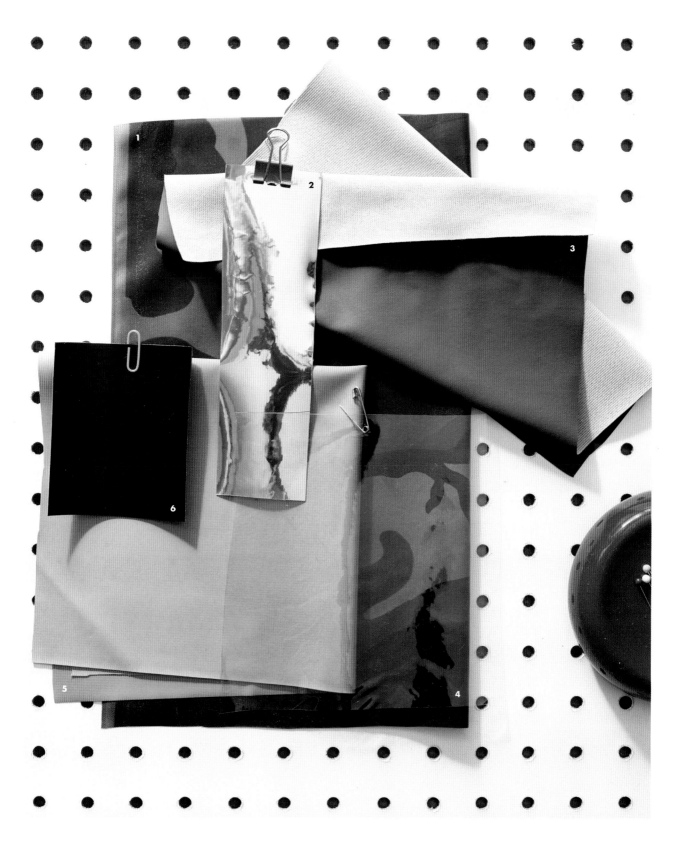

Above: Neoprene (folded) and craft foam in assorted colors.

FOAM

Yes, foam can be a fabric! Though in fashion applications it's commonly fused to other fabrics to make it look and feel better—**neoprene** being the most common example—some foams are sold as-is on the roll. Foam is generally used for industrial applications or as interlining to pad a garment, accessory, or item of home decor. **Craft foam** is also sold by the roll and can be used for all sorts of decorative and padding purposes. More adventurous designers could, in theory, make garments out of it (just don't expect a foam dress to be the most practical of pieces).

(TIPS)

- Use only thin sheet foam in a sewing machine; otherwise, you're likely to break it. Test-sew carefully and slowly, as this type of material can unduly strain a home sewing machine.

- Test thread and presser foot tension before having a go at cut pattern pieces. Foam can be tricky to get right.

- Use at least a medium-sized needle, and test different needle styles.

- If your machine won't sew sheets of foam, opt for Fabri-Tac or other fabric glue.

- With simpler styles, such as the back side of a backpack, you can also sandwich foam between fabric layers, and stitch around, rather than through, it.

"Neoprene makes for a statement piece but ensures comfort all at the same time."

—JASON WU

NONWOVEN INTERFACING

If you don't use silk organza or stiff cotton as a sew-in interfacing to stabilize sensitive areas of a garment, you can also use specially designed interfacing. Made from mashed synthetic fibers, interfacing comes in both fusible and sew-in varieties, and is made for knits or woven fabrics in a variety of weights so that you can choose the perfect one for your project. **Fusible interfacing** is designed to bond to the fabric before sewing. **Sew-in interfacing** can be pinned along the seam allowance or basted to the body fabric, but will only be attached at the seams. These fabrics are designed for a specific purpose—to be hidden and provide support—so

it's not really recommended that you use them for anything else (such as, say, a dress). They would neither last long nor feel good against the skin.

(TIPS)

- Always choose an appropriate interfacing for your project's fabric. Choose one that's close to the same thickness and weight of your fabric, or slightly thinner; use stretch for stretch fabrics and non-stretch for non-stretch fabrics (and be sure to cut the interfacing so the stretch corresponds to the fabric's stretch). To test the weight, drape the fashion fabric over the interfacing and see how the hand is affected. Be sure to make a fused sample, as well, since fusing often results in a slightly stiffer hand.
- Preshrink all interfacings. For fusibles, soak the interfacing, folded, in a basin of hot water until the water cools. Wrap the interfacing in a towel and gently squeeze out the excess water, then hang the interfacing to dry.
- Choose black interfacing when working with dark fabrics, white for lights.
- Follow the manufacturer's instructions for applying fusibles. Always use a press cloth when fusing, to keep your iron clean, and lift and lower—don't glide—the iron on the fabric.

INTERLINING
(SEE PHOTO PAGE 171)

Like interfacing, **interlining** is not meant to be seen, but serves an important function. In the case of interlining, that's usually to provide padding or warmth (or both) in outerwear, or along sensitive areas, such as the straps and back of a backpack. Types of interlining include lofty fabrics like flannel and fleece, as well as batting.

Batting is basically the inside of quilting—sheets of soft, lofty fuzz that provide warmth when used between layers of fabric. Batting is usually either bonded (the fibers are held together with resin or other bonding agent) or needlepunched (the fibers are interlaced through a process in which the batting is punctured by hundreds of needles). Bonded batting "beards" less, typically—that is, the fibers don't migrate through the outer fabric layers of your garment. You'll find batting in many weights and fiber types, including polyester, wool, cotton, and blends. For garments, wool batting is dreamy—warm, breathable, supple, and lightweight. If you want to make your own quilting, you'd purchase batting and sandwich it between two layers of fabric, then topstitch your design.

(TIPS)

- Preshrink interlining before cutting. For batting, check the manufacturer's recommendations for laundering.
- Pin or baste interlining to the outer garment fabric pattern pieces before sewing. Having interlining shift during sewing will throw off your entire piece.
- After sewing seams, trim interlining from the seam allowances, close to the seamline, to reduce bulk.

QUILTING

Quilting is a multi-layered fabric that contains lofted fiberfill sandwiched between two layers of fabric, which are stitched together in various patterns. Some quilting is designed to be used as the body of a garment, with fashion fabric on both sides; other types of quilting are intended for use as **interlining**, meant to be hidden between the outer layer of a garment and the lining. Interlining quilting generally has a white, fibrous surface and somewhat rough texture similar to that of interfacing.

(TIPS)

• Quilting can create awkward situations at seams. Use as few seams as possible in your design. If the garment won't have an additional lining, enclose seams and hem edges with bias tape.

• If using quilting on the outside of a garment, take care when laying out pattern pieces that the quilting pattern matches on adjoining sections.

• Test thread and presser foot tension on scraps before sewing pattern pieces. Use at least a medium-sized needle.

Above (top to bottom): Prequilted interlining in white, prequilted fabric for body of garment in pink and red.

Photo credits

All photographs by Johnny Miller except:

PAGE 10: Photo: Scott McDermott

PAGE 20: Photos by Barbara Nitke, Courtesy of Lifetime/*Project Runway* © 2015 A & E Television Networks, LLC. All Rights Reserved

PAGE 22: Photos clockwise from top left: David McCabe/*Mademoiselle*; © Condé Nast; Alexis Dahan/Indigitalimages.com/© Style.com; Bert Stern/*Vogue*; © Condé Nast; courtesy of Elena Salmistraro

PAGE 24: Umberto Fratini/Indigitalimages.com/© Style.com

PAGE 25: Photo: Evan Browning

PAGE 26: © firstVIEW.com

PAGES 30-31: From left to right: © riedochse/depositphotos.com; © Immfocus/depositphotos.com; viledevil/depositphotos.com; Melvyn Longhurst/SuperStock

PAGES 32-33: From left to right: © Ad Meskens/Wikimedia Commons; Nylon by DuPont Advertisement: Advertising Archive/Everett Collection; James Dean: Courtesy Everett Collection; Two for the Road: ©20th Century Fox/Courtesy Everett Collection; *Saturday Night Fever*: © Paramount/Courtesy Everett Collection

PAGES 36-38: © firstVIEW.com

PAGE 52: Bottom left: Esta Nesbitt fashion illustrations, New School Archives and Special Collection, The New School, New York, NY; bottom right: John Rawlings/*Vogue*; © Condé Nast

PAGE 58: Photo: Tommy Clark

PAGE 60: Fernanda Calfat/Getty Images Entertainment/Getty Images

PAGE 61: © firstVIEW.com

PAGE 63: clockwise from bottom left: Armani: Tim Jenkins/ *WWD*; Donna Karan: David Turner/*WWD*; Geoffrey Beene: Nick Machalaba/*WWD*; Rei Kawakubo: Thomas Iannoccone/*WWD*; Coco Chanel: Henry Clarke/ *Vogue*; © Condé Nast; Alexander Wang: Kyle Ericksen/*WWD*

PAGE 67: Annie Hall/Courtesy Everett Collection

PAGE 77: © firstVIEW.com

PAGE 83: © firstVIEW.com

PAGE 92: Coco Chanel: CSU Archives/Everett Collection

PAGE 104: © firstVIEW.com

PAGE 111: Nick Machalaba/*WWD*

PAGE 121: Pierre Schermann/*WWD*

PAGE 127: Frances McLaughlin-Gill/*Vogue*; © Condé Nast

PAGE 129: Jean Harlow/Courtesy Everett Collection

PAGE 134: © firstVIEW.com

PAGE 143: Constantin Joffé/*Vogue*; © Condé Nast

PAGE 151: © firstVIEW.com

PAGE 160: © firstVIEW.com

Quote Sources

CHAPTER 2: SOCIAL FABRIC

PAGE 25: "Looking Ahead: The Collections That Count." *Vogue.* January 1995. Voguepedia.

PAGE 27: Kors, Michael. Twitter post. April 22, 2013, 11:30 a.m., http://twitter.com/michaelkors.

CHAPTER 3: FABRIC 101

PAGE 37: Golbin, Pamela. Madeleine Vionnet. New York: Rizzoli, 2009.

PAGE 51: Ramey, Joanna. "The Toledos Live in a Glass House." *WWD.* August 28, 2009. http://www.wwd.com/eye/design/the-toledos-live-in-a-glass-house-2250736.

CHAPTER 4: FABRIC AND DESIGN

PAGE 54: Springsteel, Lisa. *Becoming a Fashion Designer*. New York: Wiley, 2013.

PAGE 57: Golbin, Pamela. *Madeleine Vionnet*. New York: Rizzoli, 2009.

PAGE 61: Bowles, Hamish. "Elsa Schiaparelli and Miuccia Prada: Talk to Her." *Vogue.* May 7, 2012. http://www.vogue.com/865351/elsa-schiaparelli-and-miuccia-prada-talk-to-her/

PAGE 62: Livingstone, David. "Fashion: Anna Sui, Where Passion and Playfulness Intersect." *Toronto Star*. October 5, 2011. http://www.thestar.com/life/fashion_style/2011/10/05/fashion_anna_sui_where_passion_and_playfulness_intersect.html.

PAGE 63:

ALEXANDER MCQUEEN Vernon, Polly. "God Save McQueen." *Guardian.* February 8, 2003. http://www.theguardian.com/theobserver/2003 feb/09/features.magazine117.

GIORGIO ARMANI "Q&A: Giorgio Armani." CNN.com. October 3, 2006. http://edition.cnn.com/2006/TRAVEL/06/01/milan.qa/.

DONNA KARAN Feitelberg, Rosemary. "Donna Karan Talks Career, Marriage and Barbra at 92Y." *WWD.* January 17, 2012. http://www.wwd.com/fashion-news/fashion-features/donna-karan-gets-grilled-at-92y-5494041.

ALEXANDER WANG von Furstenberg, Diane. "Alexander Wang Gang." *Interview* magazine. March 2010. http://www.interviewmagazine.com/fashion/alexander-wang/.

GEOFFREY BEENE Rayner, Polly. "Body of Work for 30 Years, Designer Geoffrey Beene Has Designed Clothing Without Compromise." *The Morning Call*. July 17, 1994. http://articles.mcall.com/1994-07-17/features/2996190_1_geoffrey-beene-fashion-institute-design.

YOHJI YAMAMOTO Wenders, Wim. "Yohji Yamamoto." *Interview* magazine. http://www.interviewmagazine.com/fashion/yohji-yamamoto-1#_.

KARL LAGERFELD Cowles, Charlotte. "Karl Lagerfeld on Diets, Sobriety, and Becoming a 'Nicer Person.'" *New York Magazine* The Cut. November 7, 2013. http://nymag.com/thecut/2013/11/lagerfeld-on-diets-and-becoming-a.html. Quote is from conversation between Jessica Chastain and Karl Lagerfeld.

COCO CHANEL Garelick, Rhonda. "Coco Chanel and Contagious Celebrity." In *Chanel*, edited by Harold Koda and Andrew Bolton, 22-25. New York: Metropolitan Museum of Art, 2005.

REI KAWAKUBO Kaiser, Amanda. "Rei Kawakubo on the Record." *WWD.* January 4, 2011. http://www.wwd.com/fashion-news/fashion-features/rei-kawakubo-on-the-record-3411195#/article/fashion-news/rei-kawakubo-on-the-record-3411195?full=true.

RALPH LAUREN "New Fashion Ads: The Provocative Sells." *New York Times*. April 19, 1986.

CHAPTER 5: COTTON, LINEN, AND HEMP

PAGE 66: Dove, Rachel. "The Knowledge: J. Crew's Jenna Lyons on How to Work Winter Layers." *Telegraph.* December 1, 2013. http://fashion.telegraph.co.uk/news-features/TMG10478069/The-Knowledge-J-Crews-Jenna-Lyons-on-how-to-work-winter-layers.html.

PAGE 74: Clarke, Mary. "Marc Jacobs, 2001." *Index Magazine*. http://www.indexmagazine. com/interviews/marc_jacobs.shtml.

PAGE 82: Stanfill, Francesca. "A Vision of Style." *New York Times*. September 14, 1980.

PAGE 87: "Q&A with Stella." Stella McCartney. http://www.stellamccartney.com/experience/us/ stellas-world/sustainability/stella-interview/.

CHAPTER 6: WOOLS

PAGE 90: "Next Generation Impresses at New York Shows." The Woolmark Company. March 2012. http://www.woolmark.com/mediareleases/ mr-next-generation.

PAGE 101: "Next Generation Impresses at New York Shows." The Woolmark Company. March 2012. http://www.woolmark.com/mediareleases/ mr-next-generation.

PAGE 104: "Next Generation Impresses at New York Shows." The Woolmark Company. March 2012. http://www.woolmark.com/mediareleases/ mr-next-generation.

PAGE 107: Long, Carola. "Hubert de Givenchy: 'It Was Always My Dream to Be a Dress Designer.'" *Independent*. June, 7 2010. http:// www.independent.co.uk/life-style/fashion/ features/hubert-de-givenchy-it-was-always-my- dream-to-be-a-dress-designer-1993047.html.

CHAPTER 7: KNITS

PAGE 111: Long, Carola. "Wrap Superstar: Designer Diane von Furstenberg Tells Her Story." *Independent*. March 27, 2008. http://www. independent.co.uk/life-style/fashion/features/ wrap-superstar-designer-diane-von-furstenberg- tells-her-story-801189.html.

PAGE 112: Morris, Bernadine. "Stretch Fabrics Make Fashion Comfortable." *New York Times*. May 5, 1987. http://www.nytimes. com/1987/05/05/style/stretch-fabrics-make- fashion-comfortable.html.

PAGE 115: Menkes, Suzy. "Madame Grès as Sculptor." *New York Times*. April 18, 2011. http://www. nytimes.com/2011/04/19/fashion/19iht-fgres19. html.

CHAPTER 8: SILKS

PAGE 126: The House of Herrera. Carolina Herrera, 2012. http://asp-es.secure-zone.net/v2/ index.jsp?id=5321/8405/23953&startPage=41.

PAGE 131: Morris, Bernadine. "From Mary McFadden, Two Decades of Fashion." *New York Times*. June 11, 1989. http://www.nytimes. com/1989/06/11/style/life-style-from-mary- mcfadden-two-decades-of-fashion.html.

CHAPTER 9: OTHER FABRICS

PAGE 151: Bowles, Hamish. "Elsa Schiaparelli and Miuccia Prada: Talk to Her." *Vogue*. May 7, 2012. http://www.vogue.com/865351/elsa-schiaparelli- and-miuccia-prada-talk-to-her/.

PAGE 154: Menkes, Suzy. "Taking China: Vera Wang's Long March." *New York Times*. January 10, 2006. http://www.nytimes.com/2005/11/07/ style/07iht-fwang.html.

PAGE 159: "Shop-house: Tips on the Shop Market." *Vogue*. Oct. 1, 1934.

PAGE 166: "Q&A with Stella." Stella McCartney. http://www.stellamccartney.com/experience/us/ stellas-world/sustainability/stella-interview/.

PAGE 170: Verner, Amy. "California Dreaming: Spring Fashion's Awash with Neoprene." *Globe and Mail*. March 24, 2012. http://www.theglo- beandmail.com/life/fashion-and-beauty/fashion/ california-dreaming-spring-fashions-awash- with-neoprene/article535521/.

Index

What started as a part-time job during his time at the Fashion Institute of Technology has turned into a career as manager of the home décor department at Mood. "I started in the silk department in 2008, and then I slowly came down here," he says. "I definitely like it down here a lot more. It's calmer and more intimate. "You get to meet a lot of interesting people who are doing a lot of cool projects. I like to do my own stuff and I always help out friends."

There's no normal day at Mood, he says. "It's fun. Every day is different."

DIANE PATTEN

Cashier, Mood NYC

Hometown:
North Bergen,
New Jersey

Favorite fabric:
Upholstery fabrics.
"I worked in a home
decorating store for
eight years, and I like
making stuff for my
house, and I like the
designs of it. They're
usually easy to work
with compared to silks
and slippery, kind of
crazy fabrics."

If you look to your
right when you step
through the doors of
Mood, you can't miss
Diane. She's behind
the front desk, ringing
up orders, answering
phones, and trouble-
shooting any problems.
She's constantly busy.
"If you're working at
Mood, and you're not
working hard, then
you're not working at
Mood" is her motto.
"[Fabrics] just make me
happy. It's fun to come
to work everyday."

This love of fabrics
has informed Diane's
career for more than
30 years. Following
high school, she was
hired as a trainee at
an emblem company
in New Jersey, and
eventually found
herself as an embroi-
dery enlarger at Shiftly
Embroidery, where
she drew patterns
for production for 25
years. After her work
was outsourced over-
seas, she got a job at
a fabric store in New
Jersey, then made her
way to Mood, where
she is a staff and
customer favorite. A
longtime fan of *Project
Runway*, she finds it a
bit surreal that she
can sometimes now
be seen on it.

"I just got sucked in," Sharon says. "I fell in love with the store and the fabric and the fashion even though I have no background in fabric or fashion." Sharon started out doing administrative contract work and now she knows and does everything and anything. Her education was on the job— "I'm a fast learner. If I'm around something, I learn it quickly."

Sharon loves the diversity of the Mood customers and especially enjoys getting to know the students, helping them choose fabrics for their first projects and then watching as they graduate and become full-fledged professional designers.

//////////////////////////////////////

MISHA MILLSAP

Sales Associate, Mood Los Angeles

Hometown:

Los Angeles, California

Favorite fabric:

Stretch jersey. "It's so forgiving—you can always take it in, or let it stretch out, and if you make a pattern that's too small, well, you get a sexy tight look."

//////////////////////////////////////

A home sewer since the age of seven (she learned by watching her grandmother), Misha got her first taste of the fashion industry as a teenager when she was tapped by a modeling scout. In the '80s, she walked the runways in New York, Paris, Milan, and Tokyo. "It was not a good time for fashion," she says with a laugh. Eventually returning to her hometown, Misha began styling for commercials and music videos as well as a few movies (though "nothing worth mentioning," she says). Now a mother of four, Misha is an impossible-to-miss presence at the L.A. store, thanks to her funky style and enthusiastic demeanor. And although she works with celebrities and their costumers every day, she won't name names. "Put it this way," she says. "Every time I turn on the TV or look at a magazine, I see a fabric I sold."

A ride up to the third floor in Mood NYC's famous hand-operated elevator leads to a world of fine fabrics and trims, sold by the most knowledgeable staff in the business.

Acknowledgments

The Sauma family would like to thank writer Eviana Hartman for her hard work and dedication in bringing this book to life. Her translation of Mood's history and her research of textiles have enlightened us all.

The photo team would also like to thank the following for all of their assistance during the photo shoot for this book:

Julie Batkiewicz	Dennis "Kojo" Menka
Dionisio Brown	Tarek Mohammed
Dmitry Byalik	Sharon Nunez
Kendryll Clemons	Diane Patten
George Coleman	Eric M. Perryman
Kway Collins	Wira Quesada
Melissa Dimicioglu	Juan Carlos Rios Negron
Stephanie Espinal	Alberto Rivera
Noel Francis	Anita Rivers
Denis Grams	Eileen Santos
Rochelle Hain	Betty Solomon
Kabba Jaiteh	David Steinberg
Rodhia Joseph	Lina Suriel
Todd Kelly	Richard Thomas
Mabelline Leon	Joe Varon

And finally this book is a thank you to all the employees, vendors, and most importantly customers who helped to build Mood into what it is today, and to our wives and children who support us and give us the inspiration to keep on driving forward. Never stop living your dreams and trying to make everyday better than yesterday.